Planetary Cycles Mundane Astrology

Planetary Cycles
Mundane Astrology

André Barbault

Les cycles planétaires, astrologie mondiale
Translated by Kate Johnston

The Astrological Association

Original French language edition published 2014
Under the title *Les cycles planétaires Astrologie mondiale*

This English language edition first published 2016
with kind permission of the author, under the title
Planetary Cycles Mundane Astrology
by The Astrological Association CIO,
BCM 450, London WC1N 3XX.
© The Astrological Association CIO 2016

Translation by Kate Johnston
Editor and layout: Roy Gillett
Cover design: Catherine Keane

The author has asserted his right to be identified as the author of this work in accordance with the Copyright Designs and Patents Act 1988

A catalogue record for this book is available from the British Library
ISBN 978-0-9502658-9-6

All rights reserved.
No part of this publication may be reproduced or utilised in any form or by any means electronic or mechanical, including photocopying, recording or any information, storage and retrieval system now known or hereafter invented without the prior permission of the publisher.

Printed and bound by Lightning Source

Editor's Preface

In June 2014, André Barbault, then in the second half of his 94th year, brought together the essence of eight decades of rigorous detail, relating astro-cycles to centuries of history.

Readers of his *The Value of Astrology* will know of André's refusal to be a cherry-picking astrologer. In Chapter 7, after explaining his basic methods, he writes:

> I have chosen my work rather than someone else's because of the very high standards I have set myself. I came to astrology at a very young age and I suffered a major setback which profoundly shook my initial faith; my disillusionment made me more critical, and since then when undertaking experimental forecasts I never do things the easy way. When undertaking an experiment the moment of truth is when a particular type of result occurs at the completion date of the configuration being tested, *and likewise all the way along the same continuous series.*[1] I had to rid myself of any illusions. My method was, if possible, to shut myself away in a remote faraway place where I couldn't guess at what was going on in the world and, depending only on the astronomical ephemerides, assign dates to history sometimes years and even decades in advance, the forecast thus becoming a gigantic leap in anticipating the future. It was the ultimate high risk strategy.[2]

Such rigour has enabled him to describe future events with unnerving accuracy; years, even decades, in advance. In his new book he explains the methods that enabled him to foresee the changes in the Soviet Union following the death of Stalin and again its collapse in 1989-92, as well as a major world economic crisis leading up to 2010.

However, the bulk of the book does much more than this. It takes the historical records of major points of socio-economic and political change going back to the pre-Christian era, and then focuses in great detail on the last two to three hundred years. All this is compared to the conjunctions of Jupiter to Saturn, Uranus, Neptune and Pluto; Saturn to Uranus, Neptune and Pluto; Uranus to

Neptune and Pluto; and Neptune to Pluto. Also, between the conjunctions, he shows how events connect and develop in stages through any two planets' 45 °, 60 °, 120 °, 180 °, 215 °, 240 °, 300 ° and 315 ° separations; until the next conjunction, when there is another major point in history.

The outer-planets describe the circumstances behind the trends and pent up pressures that burst out into events. These events seem triggered by combinations of many planets. So, while this book focuses on the great sweeps of change indicated by outer planets, in its later chapters André does give examples of how groups of planets combine when specific events occur. The combinations can be inner planets with outer planets, and particular planets in the charts of intervening individuals or past events.

It is typical of the breadth of the man's vision that this is followed by chapters on André's well known planetary index for world events; plus another inviting the study of the relationship between the spacing of planets around the Sun and world events.

Planetary Cycles - Mundane Astrology is both a challenge to astrology's critics as well as a benchmark of the standard to which mundane astrology should be practised. Even more important is that it could bring closer the time when the value of using astro-cycles is respected, as a companion to deepen understanding and clarify judgement, when we are taking important decisions.

Roy Gillett - April 2016

Date Conventions – All dates are Christian Era CE, unless specifically marked BCE Before Christian Era.

Acknowledgements

We are especially grateful to André Barbault for generously donating to the Association the rights to translate and publish this key insight into the methods and achievements of his long life in astrology.

Great credit for making André's wisdom available to the English-speaking world in his unique style is due to the devoted translation work of Kate Johnston, who has approached the task as a painstaking labour of love.

The Astrological Association is proud to have been able to sponsor this eminent project. The Association would like to thank: Jane Struthers for her meticulous proof reading of the draft copy; Catherine Keane for her beautiful cover; Trudie Charles and Sharon Knight for their advice on design and for finding so many of those easily-missed errors; Wendy Stacey for ongoing support and especially her help with Alice Ekrek Hovanessian's excellent index; and the Astrological Association Board of Trustees for their support throughout the project. We are most grateful to Dr Richard Tarnas and Dr. Nichols Campion for reading and commenting on the pre-publication text.

«A Roy Gillett, en toute amitié
astrologique franco-britannique»
['To Roy Gillett in recognition of our special
Franco-British astrological friendship']
André Barbault

Contents

Editor's Preface	5
Acknowledgements	7
Contributors to *L'astrologue*	10
Chapter 1 - Cyclical Cosmology	11
Chapter 2 - Europe and the Jupiter-Saturn Cycle	17
Chapter 3 - The Jupiter-Uranus Cycle	39
Chapter 4 - The Jupiter-Neptune Cycle	52
Chapter 5 – The Jupiter-Pluto Cycle	63
Chapter 6 - The Saturn-Uranus Cycle	71
Chapter 7 - The Saturn-Neptune Cycle	85
Chapter 8 - The Saturn-Pluto Cycle	105
Chapter 9 - The Uranus-Neptune Cycle	113
Chapter 10 - The Uranus-Pluto Cycle	124
Chapter 11 - The Neptune-Pluto Cycle	132
Chapter 12 - The Solar Cycle	138
Chapter 13 - Cyclic Interference	143
Chapter 14 - The Cyclic Indicator	148
Chapter 15 - Astral Alignments	153
Chapter 16 - The Great Year	159
Chapter 17 - Conclusion	162
Editor's Notes	163
Index	165

I would like to honour the people below, who have honoured astrological thought by freely contributing ideas and opinions to *l'astrologue* over the eighty years I have been writing and researching astrology.   André BARBAULT - Editor in chief.
l'astrologue **Participants** (in order) :
Maurice DRUON, *Permanent secretary of the French Academy* — André PIEYRE DE MANDIARGUES, *Prix Goncourt 1967* — R.P. Michel RIQUET — Georges MATHIEU *et* André BRETON — Jean AUJAME — Maryse CHOISY — René HUYGHE *of the French Academy* — C.G. JUNG — Claude LEVI-STRAUSS *of the Collège de France* — Paul GUTH — Arnaud DESJARDINS — Jean COCTEAU *of the French Academy* — Jacques BERGIER — Françoise GIROUD, *Director of L'Express* — Lucien MALAVARD, *Prof of science at the Sorbonne, member of the Institute* — Henry MILLER — Pierre SCHAEFFER, *Director of the research department at the O.R.T. France* — Raymond SIESTRUNCK, *Prof of science at the Sorbonne* — Werner HEISENBERG, *Nobel Prize in physics* — Guy MICHAUD, *Prof at the University Paris X* — Dr Françoise DOLTO — Dr Roger MUCCHIELLI, *Honorary Professor at the University of Nice* — André FAUSSURIER, *Director of studies at the Free University of Lyon* — Paul GERMAIN, *Prof at the Sorbonne, Permanent secretary of the Academy of Science* — Gérard COUPINOT, *Assistant astronomer at the Pic du Midi* — Antoine FAIVRE, *Prof at l'École pratique des Hautes Études (Sorbonne)* — Marguerite BORDET - Francine CARON, *Lecturer at the University Rennes II* - Robert AMADOU — Georges CESBRON, *Prof and Director of the Department of Letters at the University of Angers* — Yves DAUGE, *Senior lecturer at the Academic Centre of Perpignan* — André KARATSON, *Prof at the University of Lille* — Robert BARBAULT, *Prof at the Sorbonne* — Gilbert DURAND, *Prof at the Faculté de Chambéry* — Jean RICHER, *Prof at the University of Nice* — Jacques DESPIERRE, *member of the Institute* — Jean ANOUILH *of the French Academy* — Marguerite YOURCENAR, *Prof at the University of NewYork, member of the French Academy* — Lucien BRAUN, *Prof at the University of Louvain* - Dr Jean DIERKENS, *Prof at the Mons State University and the Free University of Brussels* — Hans J .EYSENCK, *Prof at the University of London* — Z.G. WOLKOWSKI, *Lecturer at the University P. et M. Curie* — Léon-Jacques DELPECH, *Prof at the Sorbonne* - Gérard SIMON, *Prof of Philosophy at the University of Lille III* — Jean-Claude VADET, *Senior researcher at the C.N.R.S.* — Etienne GUILLE, *Prof at the University of Paris-Orsay* — Jean-Guillaume RICHARD, *Prof responsible for a seminar on the third economic cycle at the University of Paris-Dauphine* — Yves LECERF, *Prof responsible for a seminar on the 3rd cycle of ethnology at the University of Paris VII* — Charles RIDOUX, *Aggregate Prof of the University of Valenciennes.*

Chapter 1 – Cyclical Cosmology

From the starlit firmament in the vault of heaven, the spatio-temporal universe of cosmology, the cyclical phenomenon of planetary configurations holds court. The perpetual circumpolar movement of the solar system's celestial bodies is a clock beating to an astral time animated by an analogical language.

Its origins lie in the speculations of the ancients about a Great Year. For them, the zero state at the beginning of the world was symbolized by all the planets aligning in one great conjunction. This was the all-important first gathering: the common starting point for an existence of inexhaustible, successive configurations, a cyclical future without end, from whence our hold on the future is distilled. Here we have the primordial saga of the interdependence of sky, Earth and human beings.

This initial assembly is the cornerstone of annular time where, out of the forty-five cycles of the ten planets, each astral couple makes its multi-circular journey along the zodiacal path from one conjunction to the next: the infinite configurations from which historical trends develop.

Being at the heart of the solar system, we live according to the duration of astral time with its cyclical rhythms. The founder planetary cycle is a line of both time and space in the universe, its make-up responding to a historicity of equal amplitude and of a common essence here below. These planetary cycles preside over the destiny of the world with each conjunction being a homing point at the heart of the planetary whole.

Whether there is a correlation between the planets and events is judged by the content throughout the duration of the cycle: a series of stages, resting on a parallel continuum, have a common emphasis and are of the same scale: the celestial indicators are equivalent to the historical developments and there is an evolution of the similarities between the two parties.

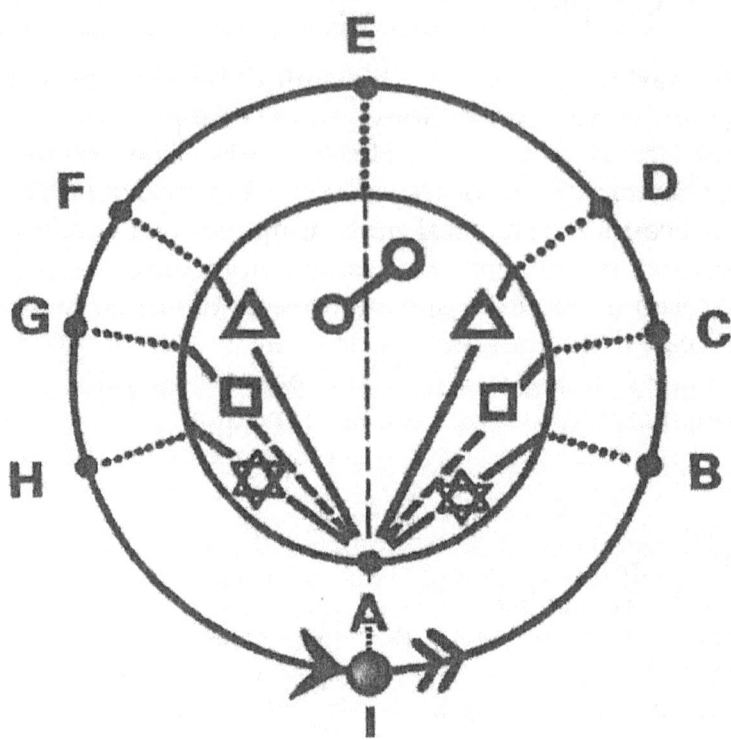

From one conjunction of the two planets to the next, the historical process follows a number of different phases which punctuate the cycle. The diagram shows the important major aspects. However, it is useful to put in some other aspects which, although called minor, are also of some importance: the semi-square (45°), the sesquiquadrate (135°) and even the semi-sextile (30°) and the quincunx (150°).

The conjunction (0°) acts as the starting point: the nascent source, germination of the seed, creative beginning. It is followed by complex developments at the semi-square (45°), growth issues. Next, at the sextile (60°), the momentum crystallizes, things start to take shape and we can see what has already been achieved. At the square (90°) there is a growth crisis due to the tension between the two factors: discord creating a climate of division or deviation from the initial direction of travel. The conflict is resolved with the fertile progressive trine (120°): this is an expansive productive phase of association or cooperation, a bringer of gains and successes. There is a boom in the wake of the cycle's ascendant phase which runs out of steam when the problems return at the disruptive sesquiquadrate (135°).

With the coming of the opposition (180°) the pendulum has swung to its highest point where the bipolar circle turns into its waning phase. This is a new turning point in its evolution: the mid-term pivotal stage, the opposite point of view to that taken at the initial conjunction, when the gains are more or less reversed as the tide ebbs. It may cause excessive risk taking. In short, it's a period of decline, of reversal or of metamorphosis. Next, the second semi-square has negative fallout, invalidating the previous gains. With the converse trine there is a return to creativity: there are new achievements and a flourishing atmosphere. The mood is more defensive or conservative than aggressive. At the square there is a new period of tension; a reassessment of what has been achieved and a risk of break-up. At the sextile, the damage is repaired, there is provisional re-structuring, a relaxation. The final semi-square often instils malaise; there is a latent crisis which more or less drags on as if waiting for the renewal at the following conjunction: the end of a complete cycle of history at the point of renewal.

In the absence of much information about these successive aspects, the opposition alone, being a radical turning point, should be enlightening: being opposite both the anterior and posterior conjunctions which frame it, there has to be a progression in the form of thesis-antithesis-synthesis, to make the cycle valid.

The nature of the phenomenon is decided by the characteristics of the two planets involved in the cycle, the sign of the zodiac against which the conjunction takes place and the changing aspects. So, for example, a Neptunian current resonates with the public mood: the ideology of the population, the collective faith of a people or some belief; and whereas Jupiter brings prosperity, Saturn relates to a hard life and to work itself. Therefore the Saturn-Neptunian current belongs to a relatively proletarian population and it's not surprising that the cycle of these two planets relates to popular revolts and also the history of communism.

Our perception is limited when it comes to the twisted helical nature of the cyclical path: the slanting furrow that forms a continuous circular loop which moves forward perpendicularly. For such a duo the uniformity of repetition is married to the diversity of the unique, the sameness of the eternal return mixing with the here and now of world landscapes that are always new. Yet, we are only able to comprehend a circular future. The arrow of time always follows the line of the orderly dialectical process: thesis-antithesis-synthesis inherent in its character. Access to a truly intelligible giver of meaning connects us, through the eternal archetypes, to the permanent order created by the repetitive nature of a revolving world.

The cycle depends on a mix of binary planets, such as the monthly lunisolar cycle that brings awareness of motherhood to the feminine world and assists in the nurturing ways of the Cancerian Moon sign. However, the intrinsic planetary revolution itself, which has its own determination, also plays its part. Thus Jupiter is related to the duration of power which is observed to follow the duodecimal rhythm of this planet. Maurice Druon made a study of this correlation by observing the reigns of around fifty royals as well as the careers of important statesmen (see 'The Fifth Republic'). The thirty year cycle of Saturn, from the awakening of puberty at its opposition to procreation around its renewal, is also clearly expressed in the periodicity of human generations.

1914-45: the cyclical path at the time of the 20 century's two world wars had a Saturnian link because Kaiser William's Saturn (Potsdam 27/1/1859, 15.00 was connected to that of Hitler (Braunau am Inn, Austria, 20/4/1889, 18.30) at 9° and 13° of Leo. The accession of the German emperor accompanied the birth of the second in a virtual relay. Then in the following cycle when the 'elder' was dethroned on 28 November 1918 (Saturn at 28° Leo), the 'younger', his future successor, receives the Iron Cross first class in August (Saturn at 14° Leo) which launches him on his conquest of power that he finally obtains at the end of the hemicycle on 30th January 1933 (Saturn at 7° Aquarius), the planet going to rejoin Leo at the end of the war.

The words below and diagram over leaflet describe an interesting case which involves a double repeat of a Saturn return, combined with a Sun-Jupiter conjunction in Cancer, giving it a territorial flavour. The following forecast made by me appeared in number 89 of 'The Astrologer' (1st trimester 1989) entitled: 'The Sun-Jupiter conjunction of 15 July 1990': *'On 30th June 1930, the last French soldiers embarked at Mainz marking the final evacuation of the Rhineland. This was a fundamental break in the history connecting Versailles (a defeated Germany) and Rethondes (a defeated France): The Sun was passing over the opposition of Jupiter in Cancer and Saturn in Capricorn. Sixty years later this phenomenon was repeated on 14-15 July 1990 when the Sun-Jupiter conjunction at 22° of Cancer falls on the MC of the foundation of the Federal Republic of Germany, and Saturn at 22° Capricorn returns to where it was when the Berlin Wall was erected (1961). All this leads to a presumption that there will be a decisive turning point for Europe which could be that of reunification of the two Germanys, although another diplomatic achievement concerning our continent can't be excluded.'* The text appeared six months before the fall of the Berlin Wall and a year and a half before the effective reunification of Germany in mid-July 1990.

Planetary Cycles Mundane Astrology

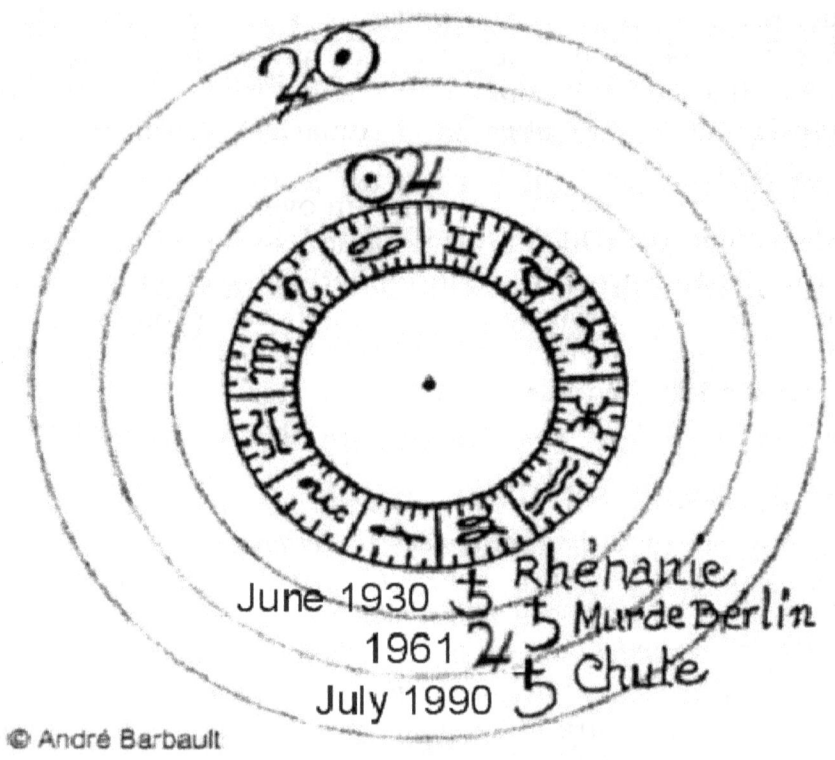

[Editor's note: Above is the author's original diagram of his prediction on the previous page, with the years inserted for: Rhénanie (France leaves the Rhineland 1930); Mur de Berlin (Berlin Wall built 1961); Chute (the Wall is torn down 1990).]

Chapter 2 – Europe and the Jupiter-Saturn Cycle

Initially, Europe's history was not tied to a destiny that was specific to one planetary cycle alone. While the national sentiments of its inhabitants were still unclear, this continent, like the rest of the world, was immersed in a planetary whole. The differentiating factor was the progress that resulted from the influence of the Renaissance which produced a more ordered society (the spread of printing, marine navigation, etc.). The continental regions (warm) influencing a group of sluggish (cold) societies, stuck in their traditional ways. The historical advances which followed placed our continent at the epicentre of human endeavour. However, this engaged us in all the contingencies of the solar system with its cyclical comings and goings.

The significant beginnings and endings in its history, and also those of other countries, respond to the rhythm of the great Uranus-Neptune cycle of 171 years. For example, the conjunction in 453 accompanied the collapse of the Roman Empire. And though that of 624, which saw the birth of Islam, was outside the continent, the following one in 793 evoked the feudal ire of Charlemagne who was crowned emperor in the year 800 just as Otto the Great was made emperor in Rome in 962, at the following conjunction. This was how Christianity gained a foothold in the medieval world, unified at its high point by the monumental structures of its prodigious cathedrals. Later on, the British monarchy took hold at the time of the Jupiter-Saturn conjunction in Virgo in 1067, the Hundred Years War (1338-1453) between France and England was framed in a Uranus-Pluto cycle, and later, the Thirty Years War (1618-1648) at the centre of the continent mirrored the Saturn-Pluto cycle.

The semi-millennium of the micro Great Year, which we are going to study, has to involve the entire solar system with all the planets returning to maximum concentration and complete cyclic renewal.

As one civilization declines (as the Roman Empire did in the east with the fall of Constantinople in 1453), another one replaces it, as happened with the creative impetus of the Italian Renaissance in the 14 century. Access to reading opened minds and the great seafarers circumnavigated all the continents: there was a general superiority of human resources in many areas and it became known as 'the civilization of western Christianity'.

Thus began the national succession of European powers. At the Uranus-Neptune conjunction of 1479, while Italy shone because of its artistic creativity, Spain, unified by the Habsburg dynasty, became the greatest power on the continent. At the following conjunction of 1649, while Holland and Sweden became great powers, it was France's turn to become the first nation of Europe.

The hegemony only expanded during the ascendant phase of the cycle, from the conjunction of 1649 to the opposition of 1734. With the Saturn-Uranus conjunction of 1761, at the Treaty of Paris, England, in its turn, became supreme in Europe, and it remained so during the whole ascendant phase of the new Uranus-Neptune cycle of 1821. British imperialism itself goes on to be supplanted by American supremacy at the Saturn-Uranus opposition of 1919.

The Jupiter-Saturn cycle
We now see the Jupiter-Saturn cycle gradually becoming established until it alone becomes specific for Europe. Its twenty year cycle was already apparent with the coronation of the Parisian Hugh Capet in 987 but we will confine ourselves to a brief summary of the 17 and 18 centuries: the arrival of Richelieu, 1643; the rise of Mazarin with the accession of Louis 14, 1663; the government of Louis XIV and the supremacy of Prussia with the accession, in 1683, of Frederic William (1640-88); the halting of the invasion of the Ottoman Turks before Vienna, 1701; the beginning of the War of the Spanish Succession and the accession of Frederick 1st 1721, king of Prussia (1713-40); the treaty of Nystad which consolidated the hegemony of Peter the Great's Russia in northern Europe, and England under Walpole

Europe and the Jupiter-Saturn Cycle

from 1721 to 1742; the beginning of the War of Austrian Succession 1741; the Treaty of Paris in 1762 and the end of the British Empire in America in 1783.

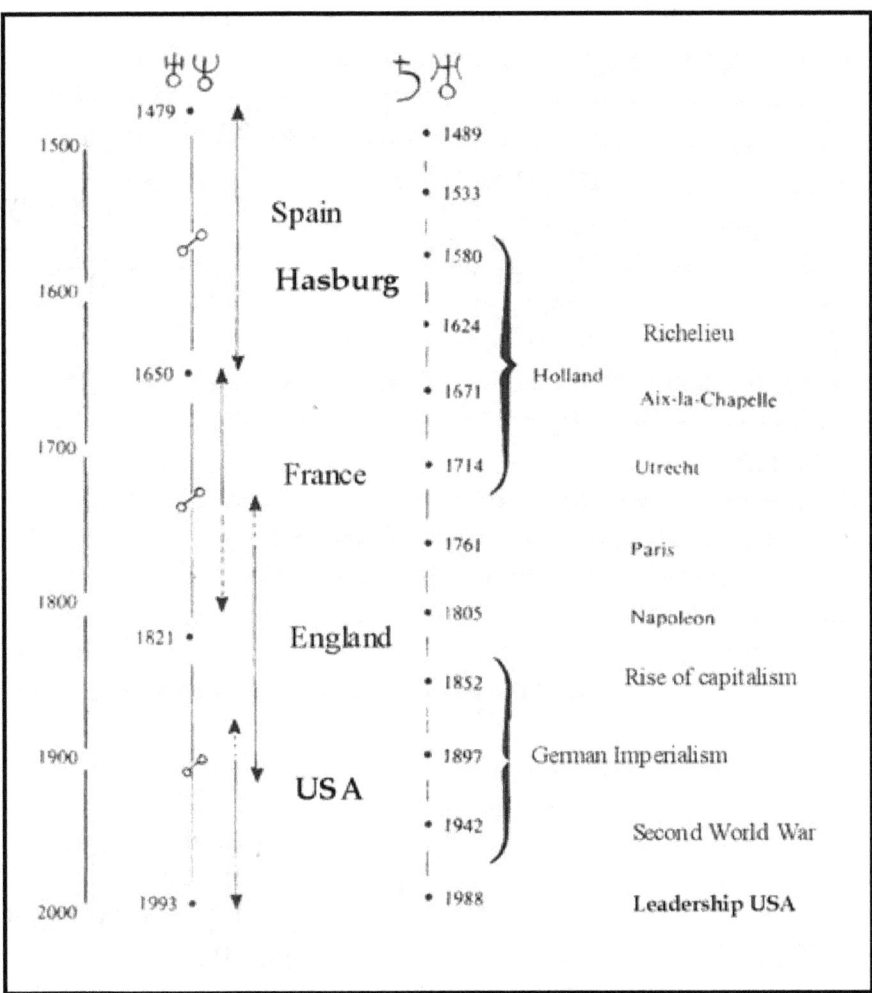

By looking at the last two centuries this investigation covers the whole of the circular pathway with an added section about Africa, as it was taken over by our continent.

Cycle 1802-21: From Napoleon to Sainte-Alliance
The years from 1802 to 1805 are covered not only by this cycle, but by a quartet made up of Jupiter-Saturn, Jupiter-Uranus, Jupiter-Neptune and Saturn-Uranus: this was a highly charged turning point in history! Throughout the course of the ascendant phase of the three most important Jupiterian cycles, Napoleon, who was made consul for life in 1802, then emperor in 1804, continued to maintain his power and to expand his empire in Europe.

The height of his power and his decline fall exactly during the three years of oppositions in the three cycles: Jupiter-Neptune and Jupiter-Uranus in 1810-11 and in 1811-12, and the Saturn-Uranus square which ended in 1816. These dissonances start with the retreat from Russia (the winter of 1812) and end with his definitive surrender and his exile in St. Helena (July 1815).

That the Jupiter-Saturn conjunction was at the beginning of Virgo (order, regulations/rules, precision, conduct, punctuality...) was significant because it saw the emergence of a new breed in society who replaced the officers and commissioners of the old regime: these were the civil servants who worked for the administration that was created under the Consulate. The public services legislated for under Bonaparte's regime were then extended to Europe and beyond. Also, he surrounded himself with a host of esteemed scholars and gave the institutionalised scientific and cultural world the growth and development it needed.

At the Jupiter-Saturn opposition of 1811-12, the victorious European sovereigns, in reaction to the spirit of the French Revolution, which had extended into the Napoleonic era, restored the old regimes throughout Europe. This conservative move was enshrined in the treaty of the Holy Alliance on 26 September1815 (trine) and the convention of Aix-la-Chapelle on 1 November 1818 (sextile) when France was returned at last to its European milieu.

Cycle 1821-41: From the Holy Alliance to Liberalism

At the conjunction, by applying the agendas agreed at the Congress of Troppau (October to December 1820), of Laibach (January to May 1821), then of Verona (October 1822), the Holy Alliance made the law of the five monarchies sovereign in Europe. In 1824 (semi-square) this order was undermined by the emergence of a new spirit: Canning brought about English withdrawal and became closer to the United States, whose message of 2 December 1823 (the Monroe doctrine) was the first to throw down a challenge to the Holy Alliance: the recognition of the new Latin American states. However, at the sextile the counter-revolution was fortified (1824-25) by the accession of Charles X of France (September 1824), albeit with weakened powers.

It is not possible to separate the opposition of 1831-32 from the Jupiter-Neptune and Jupiter-Uranus conjunctions of 1830-31. At this point a rigid conservative Europe flipped over to the side of the European revolutionary movements of the time. This was a high point of radical change that upheld liberalism and nationalism. Together with Serbian autonomy (February 1830) and Greek independence (War of Independence in March 1821), Belgian neutrality was established in January 1831. Portugal, Spain and Switzerland then liberated themselves in their turn. Under this opposition Europe was torn between reaction and liberalism.

Cycle 1841- 61: The victory of Liberalism and the advent of Italy

The liberal movement which began during the preceding cycle prevailed in some parts of the continent, creating cohesion among Western European states. In 1840 Frederick-William IV came to power in Prussia and Guizot established his authority in France. National movements were starting to emerge. From 1839 onwards scientific conferences met in Italy. They were nationalist in character and they stimulated a patriotic awakening. In 1840 there was a great surge of nationalism which spread to the small German states and also to Scandinavia. From 1842 Poland was also affected.

Prussia too was encouraged by the promises of its new king, while from 1843 onwards clandestine movements started to appear. Faced with the absolutist states of Russia, Prussia and Austria, Western Europe took shape and led by example. At the sextile of 1844-45 the Anglo-French Entente Cordiale was born. It was called into question at the square of 1846 by the complications caused by Spanish marriages; but despite the quarrels the two nations were brought together by their common interests, especially at the trine in 1848 when Europe was bolstered on all sides by national movements.

At the opposition, which lasted from November 1850 to September 1852, having just gone through an explosive revolutionary crisis the national movements paused for breath. Having come to power in France on 2 December 1850, Napoleon III renewed the Entente Cordiale and revived the European movement. In Italy, Victor-Emmanuel II made Cavour his minister (2 October 1850), then his President of the Council (November 1852), placing him on the rungs to power and immediately raising the question of Italian unity. This at a time when Prussia and Austria became firm enemies: February 1853, the Prussian commercial treaty with Zollverein was renewed and this initiated the birth of Germany under the aegis of Prussia.

Under the trine of 1855, the European dynamic revolved around the Entente Cordiale, which was endorsed by the Congress of Paris (February 1856). Liberalism took hold in the Balkan countries and also in Turkey and Greece. Then at the sextile in July 1858, at Plombières France, Napoleon III gave encouragement to the Italian movement, which, however, suffered a setback at the semi-square in September 1859.

At the conjunction, Italy became a country with its own parliament and king (early 1861) and Germany began to take shape when William I came to the throne (January 1861) and ismarck came to power (September 1862). Liberalism now reigned and there was a Franco-English trade treaty in

January 1860, which was the start of advantageous reciprocal trade between the western and central states of Europe.

Cycle of 18-81: The creation of Germany

At this conjunction, France being in a pre-eminent position on the continent, it was not only Prussia which took part in the conquest of Germany; free trade applied not only to the economy but to politics with the spread of political liberalism. There were parliamentary regimes that were more or less democratic in England, Belgium and Italy; likewise in France when, in April 1861, the authoritarian empire of Napoleon III became less restrictive with its liberal constitution. Austria, too, from March 1860, abandoned authoritarianism in its empire and also adopted a liberal constitution, Spain became more open, and autocratic Russia abolished serfdom (March 1861).

This Europe faced its first crisis at the end of the Austro-Prussian war, when the square was within orb, when the defeat at Sadowa (June-July 1866) left a weakened Austria. Under the opposition there was a huge crisis (August 1870-June 1871) with the Franco-Prussian War of July 1870 ending with the German Empire being proclaimed at Versailles in January 1871. In addition, 1870 marked the defeat of the liberals in Belgium, while Bismarck embarked on his 'Kulturkampf' and at the second square of 1875-76 imposed a Bismarckian hegemony with the Russo-Turkish War in the Balkans (1876-77); at the sextile, in July 1878, the Congress of Berlin resolved various European questions (notably the independence of Serbia). France was then reintegrated into the European mainstream with Germany at the centre.

Cycle from 1881-01: German dominance

Conjunction : Europe submits to Bismarck's Reich: The Iron Chancellor, who, in October 1879, brought about the Austro-German Alliance, then triumphed with the '*Pax germanica*' in June 1881 by building an alliance between the three Emperors (Germany-Austria-Russia), then there was the

Triple Alliance (Germany-Austria-Italy) in May 1882, a masterpiece of European diplomacy. Romania, Serbia, Greece and even Turkey were all drawn to this bloc. Berlin had all European diplomacy in its wake. In 1881, French intervention in Tunisia led to an era of colonial conquests.

Semi-square (August 1883): the first colonial ills. England's occupation of Egypt in September interfered with her relations with France and Germany.

Sextile (September 1884, exact in April 1885): The Act of Berlin. In April 1884, Bismarck launched his empire's colonial policy by establishing a German protectorate of south-western African territories, while England set about settling the question of the Suez Canal. A conference was convened in November 1884 which resulted in the Act of Berlin (26 February 1885). This established the rights of the competitors taking part in the international carve-up of black Africa.

Square (January 1886-August 1887): Crisis in Europe. 1887 was the most critical since the Franco-German War of 1870-71. First, a crisis erupted in Bulgaria in the summer of 1886 which strained relations between Russia and Austria and reduced the Alliance of the Three Emperors to the Russo-German 'Reinsurance' Treaty of June 1887. Secondly and more importantly, in 1886, France was overtaken by the fever of Boulangisme, a political movement that wanted revenge and was ready to do battle with Germany. With the two countries on the brink of war, an incident at the frontier in the spring of 1887 made Europe tremble. In addition, Bismarck dissolved the Reichstag in January 1887 and there was deterioration in Franco-Italian relations.

Trine (all of 1888 and close to October 1889): Peace. In December 1887, a Mediterranean Triple Alliance with England, Germany and Italy united in maintaining the status quo for a further five years. To reinforce his Triple Alliance, Bismarck made approaches to England and even offered an alliance against France which had returned to calm (General Boulanger was removed in March 1888 and Paris mounted a brilliant world exhibition in 1889.

Opposition (April 1891-March 1892): Franco-Russian duplicity and Weltpolitik. In 1891 Russia reneged on the understanding it had with Germany and began negotiations with France. The resulting Accord which, in principle, sanctioned a reversal of the Russo-German alliance concluded in August 1891 and was signed in August 1892. It was a duplicitous arrangement. The Accord wrested the continent from German hegemony and laid the foundations for a new balance in Europe. This opposition somewhat expunged the preceding one, in 1871, when France was defeated. Apart from that, Bismarck, having come to power at the preceding conjunction, was returned in March 1890, leaving Germany at the height of its economic expansion with Weltpolitik employed all across the world, at the mercy of all its dangers.

Semi-square (June 1893-May 1894): The year of 1893 was dominated by Franco-English tension over Siam.

Trine (June 1894-May 1895): The rise of imperialism. England under Joseph Chamberlain conquered more territory (the taking of South Africa). In Russia the empire of the Tsars was enlarged by expanding into China. Also, in 1895, Berlin intervened in the Far East and the Peking convention (November 1895) gave Germany, Russia, France and Japan responsibility for China. After the division of Africa, that of Asia was now sketched out.

Square (July 1896 and closer in April 1897): Various rivalries. New conflicts in the East. The Greco-Turkish war in April 1897. In March 1896, Italy attacked Abyssinia and suffered defeat at Adwa. In the same month England set out to conquer Sudan, stirring up rivalry with the French. This led to the Fachoda incident the following year.

Sextile (October 1897-August 1898): Anglo-German detente. In 1898 came a first attempt at Anglo-German rapprochement; an agreement was reached about the Portuguese colonies in August 1898. The Anglophobia current in France decreased and there was even a relaxation in Franco-German relations. Furthermore, on 24 August

1898, Russia invited the European powers to an international conference with a view to ending the arms race.

Semi-square (November 1898- August 1899): The Boers and Fachoda. The rapid fall of the Pacific wave: the peace conference at The Hague May to July 1899 was cut short. In June the Boer war started, then in October, the Transvaal War, and on 27 October 1898 the French army evacuated Fachoda and abandoned its attempt to conquer the Nile. Franco-British tension was at its height.

Conjunction: The decline of German hegemony. The Boxer Rebellion in the spring of 1900 united German, French, Russian and English interests when, fighting side by side, they imposed a protocol on China (Sept-ember 1901) neutralising their divergent interests: this was the first truly European act vis-à-vis a country on a foreign continent. German hegemony still prevailed but the Triple Alliance, created at the previous conjunction, declined. There were Austro-Hungarian internal difficulties and the secret Franco-Italian Accord of December 1900 with the visit of the Italian navy to Toulon in April 1901.

The conquest and division of Africa (1882-1902)

The African continent became resigned to the intervention of European countries all through this cycle as *The History of Africa* by R and M. Cornevin (Payot 1964) shows:

> This chapter could be titled: 'The twenty years that made the Africa of today', because if a new map of Africa had been drawn in 1902 it would have been totally different from that of 1882. Instead of a coastal strip barely occupied by Europeans except in South Africa and Algeria, it would show the whole of the colonized continent in brush strokes of various colours representing the colonial possessions of eight European powers England— France, Germany, Portugal, Belgium, Italy, Turkey, Spain, the last three only occupying a limited area. In 1902 only three African countries were still independent: Morocco, but only for ten years, Ethiopia, after being a theoretical Italian protectorate for seven years, and Liberia. The

Europe and the Jupiter-Saturn Cycle 27

map remained much the same until the First World War when the four German colonies (Togo, Cameroon, South-west and East Africa) changed colours to those of England, France and Belgium. It only changed in 1956 when Sudan, Tunisia and Morocco became independent; by 1964 it was covered in numerous colours, with thirty-three 'African' independent states, and sixteen countries that were still 'European'.

The starting gun for this colonization movement was fired (at the conjunction) when a French protectorate was imposed on Tunisia (12 May 1881). This was followed by the English occupying Egypt (13 September 1882), and France and Belgium responded by declaring the Congo their preserve. The other states expressed their concern about these actions throughout 1883. On the 24 April 1884, it was Bismarck's turn to create a protectorate on the west coast. We have reached the sextile in the cycle, reinforced by a Uranus-Neptune trine. At a conference in Berlin on 27 February 1885 the pirating of the African continent was normalised and a rush of conquerors began the next day. The conquest was completed as the cycle turned at the opposition but the downward slope was to see the birth of the principal African resistance movements which went on to liberate the continent.

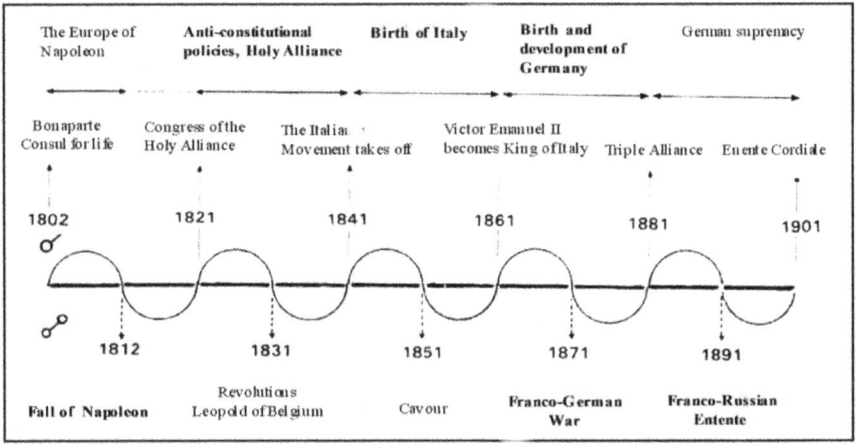

Cycle 1901-21: Improved Franco-English relations
Conjunction (November 1901): Anglo-German hostility. The German hegemony dominated the beginning of this cycle. Bismarck's successor Bulow, who became chancellor in 1900, was the arbiter of Europe, but the death of Queen Victoria (21 January 1901) put the Francophile king Edward VII on the throne and Delcassé, the French foreign minister at the Quai d'Orsay, moved closer to England and also to Italy with an accord that was finalised in 1902. Moreover, there was mounting Anglo-German tension over maritime ambitions and the last attempts at an understanding between London and Berlin vanished in October 1901 because of the South African war. This colonial rivalry, maritime and economic, between the two countries went on to dominate history.

Semi-square (June-February1903-04): Russia eliminated Russia went to war with Japan in February 1904 and was defeated. Its diplomatic influence diminished.

Sextile (May-June 1904): The Entente Cordiale. After a visit by Edward VII to Paris in May 1903 there was an Anglo-French rapprochement and on 8 April 1904 a colonial accord was signed which established the diplomatic basis of the Entente Cordiale. This was the prelude to the Triple Entente that followed.

Square (July 1905-May 1906): The Tangier crisis. In the spring of 1905, Germany contested France's attempt to establish a protectorate in Morocco. This Tangier crisis was in full swing in June-July and was only resolved with the Act of Algeciras on 7 April 1906. Aside from this climate of war, Germany sought to counterbalance the London-Paris axis by attempting to divert Russia (The Treaty of Bjorko, later disowned by the Tsar in November). In addition, there was yet another conflict between Sweden and Norway which resulted in the King of Sweden, Oscar II, being removed from the throne.

Trine (September 1906-August 1907): The Triple Entente. In January 1906 Anglo-French talks stabilized the Entente Cordiale and an Anglo-Russian rapprochement initiated in the course of 1906 resulted in a convention which concluded on 31st August 1907.

Semi-square (October 1907-August 1908): The Bosnian crisis. In the summer of 1908, problems came to a head in the Balkans and led to the Austrian annexation of Bosnia-Herzegovina in October.

Opposition (November 1910-October 1911): Agadir and the first Balkan War. In March 1911, the Moroccan affair was back in the frame with an intervention by French troops on 4 May. There was a state of alert in Europe when, on 1 July, a German warship began to cruise off the coast near Agadir. Peace didn't come until 4 November 1911. Furthermore, the first Balkan war was fought in Macedonia from 28 of September to the 3 of December 1912. The central powers only intervened in order to formulate a truce, the Balkan peninsula remaining out of bounds for the rivalries of great states. It's no surprise that with the Jupiter-Saturn opposition, augmenting a weighty Uranus-Neptune opposition Europe was massively divided by the two blocs formed by the Triple Alliance and the Triple Entente, which were always on the verge of breaking up.

Semi-square (March-April 1913): The second Balkan War. The war resumed on 3 of February and ended in August 1913, while military service was prolonged on both sides of the Rhine, as if in preparation for action.

Trine (March 1914-January 1915): resistance by the Triple Entente. After the outbreak of war in the first days of August 1914, the efforts of Great Britain, France and Russia halted the German military's rush to the gates of Paris.[3]

Square (March 1916-January 1917): Afflictions and Russian defection. The war went well for the central powers for all of 1916. Russian involvement was ineffective and soon ended; otherwise, disaffection among the troops led to the mutinies in the spring of 1917.

Sextile (June 1917-April 1918): American intervention. The United States entered the war the 2 April 1917 on the side of the Allies. This crucial contribution was to become a long-term undertaking and was most effective in the summer of the following year.

Semi-square (July 1918): Final German offensive. In mid-June, before the full American reinforcements arrived and after achieving three limited victories, Ludendorff attempted one last offensive: the new battle of the Marne, which again threatened Paris, was not successful, and led to capitulation on 11 November 1918.

Cycle of 1921-41: Versailles and European order.

Treaties were formulated between June 1919 and August 1920 (Versailles, Saint-Germain, Trianon, Neuilly and Sevres). Europe was gradually organized by London and Paris and a system of coalitions was established in central Europe (Yugoslavia and Czechoslovakia): the Little Entente (1920-22) was formed to safeguard the established order. The main instrument of this new European order was the League of Nations which was born at the Jupiter-Neptune conjunction in January 1920. The League adopted the principles of Geneva and evolved despite a lack of harmony. (Neptune semi-square to the Jupiter-Saturn conjunction.)

Semi-square (February-November 1924): An Anglo-French dual and the Ruhr. The discord between a France desirous of applying the treaties and a Great Britain which was liberal in their use soon became apparent. More importantly, since 1923, France and England had been fighting over the supply of coal. The French occupation of Ruhr was met with passive resistance which took the form of a lock-out. Also, the Nazis made their first breakthrough at the national elections in May 1924.

Sextile (February-October 1925): Locarno and the Dawes Plan. In 1924 the beginning of an Anglo-French collaboration saw Franco-German talks successfully concluded on 6 October 1925 at the conference of Locarno where the adversarial nations were on an equal footing and were attempting to live in peace. The best years were beginning for the Dawes Plan.

Square (April 1926-February 1927): Germany at the League of Nations. On 8 September 1926, Germany joined the League of Nations, but she went to Geneva to make changes, whereas France wanted to keep the status quo. Despite Briand (France) and Stresemann (Germany) getting together for secret talks at Thoiry, each stuck to their guns. Also, in April 1927, Hungry and fascist Italy signed a treaty of friendship.

Trine (June 1927-April 1928): The Paris Pact. The spirit of Locarno having returned, the conference on disarmament resumed. It went so well that on 27 August 1928, the delegates of every country in the world signed the Briand-Kellogg pact in Paris. The League of Nations was at the height of its prestige: war was outlawed and the status quo maintained. A symbol of the politics of cooperation and peace, the pact which renounced war raised huge hopes worldwide.

Opposition (July 1930-June 1931): Evacuation of the Rhineland, the Young Plan, the Hoover moratorium, suspension of payments. Nazism prevailed in Germany. The world economic crisis which started in the autumn of 1929 called everything into question and on 20 June 1931, ahead of the German financial collapse, President Hoover announced a year-long suspension of all intergovernmental payments (they were later abandoned). The Nazis were nearing power. As the Europe of Versailles reached its twenty-year milestone the ties were severed: a crucial threshold had been crossed. The first ten years of the ascendant phase of the cycle had seen reconstruction in Europe. The new era which began with the following ten years wouldl see the dismantling of the European order which arose from the First World War.

Semi-square (October 1932-September 1933): Hitler and German re-armament. The disarmament conference which began in February 1932 dragged on endlessly with no result. Having come to power in January 1933, Hitler withdrew from the League of Nations in the October and shortly afterwards launched his country on the path to unlimited rearmament.

Trine (October 1933-September 1934): The Stresa Front. In reaction a number of defensive alliances were created. The Rome Accords which concluded in January 1935 were followed, in April, by the Stresa conference which reunited France, Great Britain, Italy, the USSR and the Little-Entente; repudiating the German tactics and reasserting the obligations of Locarno.

Square (November 1935-September 1936): Italian-Ethiopian War, reoccupation of the Rhineland, Spanish Civil War. On 3 October 1935 Italy attacked Ethiopia. The war weakened the Stresa Front and led to the Rome-Berlin axis. Furthermore, on 7 March 1936 Hitler occupied the demilitarised zone of the Rhineland and prepared for the future annexation of Austria which took place on 11 March 1938. After a revolution in Spain all relationships between the European powers were overturned.

Sextile (December 1937-May 1938): Munich and Franco-British rapprochement. The Munich Accords of September 1938 were only an illusion of peace; a real agreement for a common defence was finalized between London and Paris.

Semi-square (May–December 1938): After the ;, Czechoslovakia and Memel conquered, and Albania annexed by Italy. The continent was seized by war fever, and began its descent into the savagery of the jungle.

Cycle 1940-61: From Nazi Europe to the dawn of European community.

Conjunction (August 1940–February 1941): War and the Resistance. On 9 April 1940 Germany invaded Denmark and Norway, and within two months France, Belgium, Holland and Luxemburg had also suffered military collapse. The hellish explosive nature of the Jupiter-Saturn-Uranus triple conjunction held sway. However, the Jupiter-Saturn conjunction was squared by Pluto and this undermined the Nazi victory because the violence of the assault and the atrocities committed by the dictatorship triggered the first underground resistance movements.

Semi-Square (November 1942-August 1943): The end of Mussolini and the retreat from Stalingrad sounded the death knell for Hitlerism despite the various tensions between the Allies and also within the Resistance.

Sextile (November 1943-September 1944): Continuing Nazi defeats and the Allies on the rise. In the autumn of 1944 the greater part of Europe was liberated from German occupation and in the various countries in which there was still fighting the Resistance was winning.

Square (December 1945-November 1946): The East-West divide. During 1946, with civil war in Greece and war starting in Indochina, tension in the Security Council indicated that there was a rift between Eastern and Western Europe; with the Truman doctrine in March 1947 this became entrenched; former Allies now became enemies.

Trine (January-December 1948): The Council of Europe. On 17 March 17 1948 the Treaty of Brussels was signed by France, the UK and the Benelux countries. The Congress of Europe was held in The Hague from 7 to 10 of the following May, with Churchill, Blum, Spaak and De Gasperi, with the aim of creating a democratic European Union. This was the start of the negotiations which led to the creation of the Council of Europe on 28 January 1949. It was signed at the quincunx (150°) on 5 of May, on the arrival of the De Gasperi-Schuman-Adenauer trio.

Opposition (April 1951-February 1952): the European Defence Community and the European Coal and Steel Community; a radical about-turn with the enemy, at the time of the conjunction, now becoming a friend. The return of Germany to the European fold; France rejected the idea of Germany joining the 'European Defence Community' (February 1951), because it would have implied German rearmament. At this halfway point in the cycle, Germanic integation was nevertheless successful with the Treaty of Paris (18 April 1951) establishing the 'European Coal and Steel Community', the beginning of the European Union.

Trine (June 1954-April 1955): The Western European Union (WEU). Following on from the London conference in October 1954 the Paris Accords were signed on 23 October 1955, founding the Western European Union. Moreover, a conference in Berlin in February 1954 led to the Austrian State Treaty (15 May 1955). On 1 June 1955 discussions about a common market were concluded at Messina and a committee made responsible to draft the report.

Square (August 1955-June 1956): The Suez Crisis. Numerous conferences in Geneva ended with no outcome. And, more importantly, the nationalization of the Suez Canal by Nasser in July 1956 precipitated a military intervention in Egypt on 30th October 1956: this was a fiasco and the central European states lost all influence in the Middle East.

Sextile (September 1957-June 1958: The EEC. On 25 March 1957 treaties were signed in Rome establishing the Common Market and the European Atomic Energy Community which also contributed to economic unification: The European Economic Community, 'the Six', came into force on 1 January 1958.

Cycle 1961-81: Europe and the Common Market

Conjunction (February 1961): The Common Market was established. The Treaty of Rome institutions were slowly introduced from 1959 onwards. In November 1960, the Europe of the Six was almost established and negotiations were begun for Britain to join the Common Market.

Semi-square (May 1963): First conflict. On 14 January 1963 de Gaulle spoke against future British membership and from May Franco-German relations deteriorated.

Sextile (April 1964): The European communities merge. From 1964 to early 1965, progress was made towards economic integration with the administrative merger of the three institutions: the European Community of Coal and Steel, the European Economic Community and the European Atomic Energy Community (Treaty 8 April 1965).

Square (July 1965): The agricultural crisis. Negotiations in Brussels over the financing of the Common Agricultural Market broke down on 30th June 1965. This was the most serious crisis so far for the European Community. On 1 July, Gaullist France decided to boycott proposals put forward by the commission. The brakes were applied and the political crisis continued for the rest of the year.

Trine (September 1966- July 1967): Diplomatic progress and the Common Agricultural Market. De Gaulle and Kosygin exchanged visits between July and November 1966 with de Gaulle going to Moscow and Kosygin going to Paris. This resulted in a thaw in East-West relations. The inter-European rapprochement bore fruit: the Common Agricultural policy was finally established on 1 July 1967.

Opposition (December 1969-October 1971): European rejuvenation: An East-West détente and Great Britain integrated into the Community. Supported by a Jupiter Neptune conjunction, the East-West détente which began at the trine ended in German-Soviet reconciliation (12 August 1970). This was followed by the agreement on Berlin between the four great powers and the two Germanys (3 September and 11 December 1971): On 30th June 1970 negotiations began over the enlargement of the Community with four other countries wanting to join. Great Britain, which had applied to join at the conjunction (9 August 1961), finally joined in June 1971 (integration was complicated and difficult, as Germany's had been at the preceding opposition). And although the conference at The Hague in December 1969 was to be the starting point for the Common Monetary Policy, the monetary system was plunged into crisis by the dollar becoming a 'floating currency' (15 August 1971); it was a time of huge dependency on the oil producing states (OPEC) for energy. Another sign: US troops which had remained in Europe since their military intervention finally withdrew.

Trine (February 1974-January 1975); Detente in European Council: Whereas the climate at the semi-square in 1973 had been one of monetary crisis between Europe and the US (the 'B-52s' abandoned Brussels) Euro-American relations improved greatly at the Washington Energy Conference (11-13 February 1974) and were further strengthened at the Ottawa conference (26 June 1974). With the impetus of the Copenhagen Summit (December 1973), cooperation was rewarded at the Paris Summit with the creation of the Council of Europe which, in turn, led to the European Union.

Square (May 1975-March 1976): Various troubles. The returning economic crisis disrupted the Americano-European accords and the Mediterranean basin became politically unstable: the dispute over Cyprus. There were political storms in Portugal and Spain with the deaths of Salazar and Franco; the communists made advances in Italy as did the socialist-communist union in France which went on to win at the conjunction.

Sextile (May-1977-March-1978): The ECU; reaffirmation of European economic unity leading to the Bremen Agreement in July 1978. The ECU was created to address the monetary problem and a European parliament became more imminent (semi-sextile).

Cycle 1981-2000: A laborious continental unity

Conjunction (December 1980 –July 1981): Between Euro-pessimism and continental revival. Effects: The conjunction restructures the course of history whether in schism (1940-41), in continuation (1961) or plain uncertainty. A second 'oil shock' in 1979 and East-West tensions plunged the western world into a state of fear and prompted the creation of the peace movements which were unprecedented (conjunction in Libra). Millions marched in all the western capitals as the fearful Euro missiles, the SS-20's, were deployed and Pershing missiles hovered overhead. The world was on the brink of a new world war.

The members of the European Economic Community, who had been nine in number for the past seven years, now became ten and were soon twelve. In addition, immigration was a heavy burden with too many foreigners who were becoming increasingly difficult to manage. They were also faced with a market of 320 million consumers whose standard of living had lowered.

Semi-square (January 1984): A sudden halt. After the complete failure of the 27 Council of Europe in Athens (2-6 December 1983) the British vetoed the rebalancing of community resources at the European Council in Brussels on 19th March 1984.

The problems were resolved at the Council of Fontainebleau on 26 June 1984. Next, the Six agreed on a revision of the Treaty of Rome in order to establish an 'economic area without borders' (3 and 4 December in Luxembourg).

Square (March 1984-January 1985): Transatlantic crisis. In addition to disputes over the GATT negotiations there was a deterioration in the relationship between Europe and America: the shadow of protectionism, the gas pipeline affair and the penalising of European companies.

Trine (May 1987- March 1988): Progress. On 13 June in Luxemburg the twelve finance ministers decided to release in advance the capital that they anticipated would move within the community in 1999. This measure radically dispelled any Euro-pessimism, and gave the Toronto summit in June 1988 a new vision of the European Economic Community as the world's foremost buyer.

Opposition (September 1989-July 1990): Crucial historical turning point: This configuration was out of the ordinary because the Uranus-Neptune-Saturn conjunction was opposed by Jupiter. This triad was the reason I felt justified in forecasting social upheaval with the Soviet Union at the epicentre. I made this forecast thirty years before it happened and repeated it on various occasions, either in texts or at international conferences. This, then, was the fall of the Berlin Wall on 9 November 1989 which completely transformed European society.

Next there was a Jupiter-Saturn quincunx with Saturn in a line-up of seven planets that were all within a span of about 30°. This accompanied the signing of the Maastricht Treaty on 7 February 1992 with the founding the European Union. The new Jupiter-Saturn conjunction in Taurus in 2000 saw the birth of European monetary union. While at the latest opposition of 2010-11 there had to be new critical turning point brought about by the unprecedented rout of the Euro. This substantive forecast was also made twenty years earlier in the special twenty-first century number of *L'astrologue* no. 92', 4th trimester 1990. The European continent will face another ordeal at the next conjunction of 2020-21 which also involves Pluto: a Jupiter-Saturn-Pluto triad discordantly ramified by a Uranus-Neptune semi-square does not bode well.

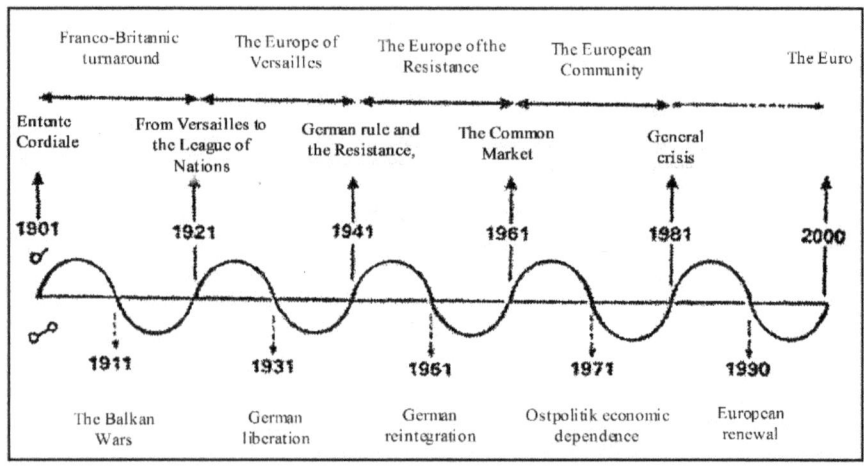

Chapter 3 – The Jupiter-Uranus Cycle

The Jupiter-Uranus synodic cycle takes 14 years to complete and because their differing speeds cause their successive conjunctions to move forwards about 60°, by the end of their 83-4 year sidereal journey round the zodiac they have inscribed a six branched star on the circle of the signs.

All civilizations alternate between times of prosperity and creativity and times of rapid decline. However, with both planets being highly charged, the tension of this conjunction can just as easily serve up the best as the disastrous worst.

In a symbolic converse drawing of the diurnal cycle, the Saturn-Neptune duo would be placed analogically at the IC opposite this planetary duo which is allied to the culmination, the MC. It has the power of a vital Air-Fire placement both in amplitude and intensity, whether applied to diehard ambition in the service of progress or to terrible depravity. A good example is the conjunction of 20 July 1969, the Apollo 11 flight; when Man set foot on lunar ground the night stars themselves aligned with this planetary duo. And conversely, the worst years, 1914 and 1941.

The French Revolution and the discovery of electricity
When it comes to unexpected events in history, nothing surpasses the thunderclap of the French Revolution on 14 July 1789: a Jupiter-Uranus conjunction at the beginning of Leo, the indulgent sign of 'me', was in a line-up with a Sun-Mercury-Venus trio and trine to a popular Moon in Aries. That day the people of Paris seized the bastion of the Bastille, the hated fortress prison: the act that started the French Revolution.

This led to the night of the 4-5 August – with a close Sun-Jupiter conjunction in Leo –when the National Assembly voted for the abolition of the feudal system of privileges! The oak tree of feudalism was felled at one stroke, putting an end to a thoUSnd years of the Middle

Ages: This was the birth of the citizen, with equality before the law for all human beings and it led, on 26 August, to the famous Declaration of the Rights of Man and of the Citizen.

And it's no surprise that, later, with his firework of a Uranus (on the Ascendant surrounded by Sun-Mercury-Venus), Max Stirner (Bayreuth, 25/10/1806, 06.00) pushed his individualism to the extreme; an eccentric to the point of being an apostle for the most radical anarchism. Another kind of extremism: the world's tallest giant, Robert Pershing Aldo (Alton/Illinois, 22/02/1818, 06.30, *Guinness Book of Records*) who was 2.72m tall. The result of having Jupiter on the IC, square to Uranus in Aquarius on the Ascendant in conjunction with Sun-Mercury-Venu. So then, with Uranus stimulated everywhere and in every way you get: excess, gigantism, extremism, immoderation, the quality of being unique. Similarly, with this planet you can get a dramatic turn of events such as terrible storms and other climatic disasters.

Uranus was discovered by Herschel in 1783. At this point we went from a latent state to one that manifests: its discovery was like that of a new planet, one that was in a higher octave with its orbit much greater than that of Saturn. This astronomical revolution occurred at the same time as the French Revolution (1789), when a Jupiter-Uranus conjunction in Leo signalled the advent of the individual, the human entity belonging to no one but itself.

Also at the same time – except for the phenomenon of the exterminating demon that failed to feed the creative genius – there was a realization of individual potential and a flood of new conquests. Previously, when the planet was in its home in Aquarius (1742-51), electricity sparked in the Leyden Jar for the first time, and lightening was channelled with Benjamin Franklin's lightening rod. When Uranus returned to Aquarius (1828-35) the electricity industry took off, with Pixii's discovery of alternating current and its conversion to continuous current by Clarke. Then there was the dynamo, the telegraph, electrolysis, electrochemistry; the supply of light, locomotives, ships, lighthouses... In short, with the Uranian expansion of the solar system, followed soon after by the discovery of Neptune, humanity moved into a new dimension responding to this cosmological expansion...

Uranian military flare-ups
But haven't we always been subject to primal Uranian forces. My early research into around sixty declarations of war, published in *The Planets and History*, led me to the conclusion that this energy comes from a large variety of configurations, each conflict being the product of a specific given. For example, for civil or revolutionary wars the energy is Neptunian, and for interventions of an imperialist nature Uranian. However, here, the Jupiter-Uranus conjunction also plays a role because in these situations Jupiter combines its taste for power with that of excessive risk taking.

It's just around the time of their conjunctions in 1845, 1858 and 1886 that you have the expeditions and colonial conquests which lead to the Europeanization of the world along with rivalries that will end up as future imperialist confrontations.

In the 20 century the correlation with warmongering is striking. With the conjunction of 1900, although we had the creation of the Commonwealth of Australia, the Boers and the Boxers began an anti-colonialist war. Then, more strikingly, with the next one in 1914 there was the sudden explosion of the First World War. And though the third conjunction of 1927-28 - a pause for breath - only saw the installation of European dictators (Poland, Lithuania, Portugal, Yugoslavia) in the wake of a hawkish right which won in all these countries, it was at the fourth in 1941 – because again in 1939-40 this was not just a European war – that the three giants intervened: USSR, US and Japan, in the Second World War.

Though less spectacular, the fifth in 1954-55 had France at the heart of wars of decolonialization, between the dramatic fall of Dien Bien Phu and the advent of the painful Algerian War. There was also the Bandung conference which brought together the Third World countries united in their wish to eliminate colonialism and the nationalization of the Suez Canal by Nasser, which the Middle East. Remember also the botched Franco-British military intervention in Suez. As for the sixth conjunction of 1968-69, at the very dawn of electronics bringing the technological prowess which put a man on the Moon, the devastating worldwide student revolt immediately comes to mind along with the military intervention of the Warsaw Pact in Czechoslovakia and the beginning of the Troubles in Northern Ireland.

The seventh conjunction of 1983 marked an ultra-critical year, a world on the brink of a third world war, with the installation of nuclear sites in Eastern Europe: Pershing and SS-20's were face to face, Euro missiles confronting each other and the extremity of the breakdown of negotiations in Geneva! Also following the Falklands War, the Persian Gulf was in flames with the Arab world in revolt in the Middle East and an American intervention with an armada of about thirty war ships (many of which were wrecked).

The eighth conjunction of 1997 was an exception; it was very unusual in that it formed a triptych with Neptune: the coming together of the three elements that accompanied the arrival of the Internet and which toppled the world into a new era. But the last conjunction of 2010 in Aries fell on the explosive Arab revolt which involved the whole of the African continent. In April 2008 I wrote a reminder on my website entitled 'May 68' in which I spoke about the risk that Libya's Colonel Gaddafi might fall in 2010 because this conjunction went on to oppose the previous Jupiter-Uranus conjunction at the beginning of Libra which occurred when he took power forty-two years earlier in 1969.

In short, you just have to look at this line-up—1914, 1941, 1968, 1983—to smell the gun powder. As for the Jupiter-Uranus oppositions, several fell at the height of tension between the three great powers: the Berlin blockade in March 1948, the first great test of power of the Cold War, and the Cuban missile crisis in October 1962 when humanity came close to a third world war. Even those that followed in

The Jupiter-Uranus Cycle

August 1975 (4° orb) and April 1976 saw the emergence of a war in Lebanon and the return of the Cold War caused by Soviet intervention in African countries, etc.

Evaluating the gravity of the danger
It would be nice to know how you could quantify the risk of explosion with such a configuration.

Firstly, you could compare the single conjunctions with the triple conjunctions caused by Jupiter turning retrograde and so extending the duration. However, the conjunctions of 1914 and of 1941 were single; it's true they were not alone, they were assisted by a Saturn-Pluto conjunction and later by the Uranus-Neptune opposition; likewise the second conjunction was joined by Saturn to form a triad. But even though those of 1927-28 and 1954-55 were repeated three times they don't seem to carry any more weight.

Likewise, we have to reluctantly give up the idea that the perfection of the phenomenon could be important. This is when the conjunction is doubled by being in parallel, at the same declination at the same time as being at the same longitude: that's to say, without latitude. Equally, whether or not this meeting or physical alignment happens to be on the ecliptic. Thus during the 20th century, the third Jupiter-Uranus conjunction of 10 May 1955 was the closest, at only 1° apart in declination and 0.5° north in latitude. While that of 1941was in the same boat as those of 1900 and 1928, being only about thirty minutes from the ecliptic. In short, this approach was also proved to be worthless, along with the research that followed into whether the planets were at perihelion or aphelion.

That leaves the sign or the location of the configuration. But here, the differences are less quantitative than qualitative. In fact it's surprising how similar the events are in nature when you compare one with another.

Thus the Uranus-Neptune conjunction at the beginning of Sagittarius back in 1479, followed by the Jupiter-Saturn conjunction in 1485, initiated an era of maritime conquests by Portuguese and Spanish navigators, which ended with the discovery of America in 1492. At the time of our Jupiter-Uranus conjunction in Sagittarius, steam navigation arrived in 1819 and in 1900 there was another transport revolution that led to aviation; also, the following year the first wireless signal crossed the Atlantic.

And while we are on the subject of locomotion, remember that between 1970 and 1988 Uranus and Neptune also travelled through Sagittarius. This turning point saw global air traffic grow to such an extent that air travel around the world became an ordinary occurrence. Not to forget manned spacecraft and also the shuttles, Salyut, Skylab... In short, humans were conquering world travel in every way. We must also mention that opposite, when Uranus was crossing Gemini, the era of the private motor car began, which transformed the way we travel. After the devastation of the world war the production of a record number of cars in the United States provided a compensatory kickstart to the economy. Production multiplied eightfold between 1945 and 1950 and Western Europe followed suit. To this can be added the advent of television, which transformed the home with its abundance of broadcast images, sounds and words. Plus, under the third conjunction in Sagittarius of 1983, outer space became crowded with an arsenal of spacecraft which more than ever revolutionised human exchange and, thanks to which, the Internet was born.

There is no doubt that the planet takes on the nature of the zodiacal sign it is passing through. The case of Lavoisier stands out: as Uranus crossed Gemini in 1777 he identified the presence of oxygen in air; when in Cancer in 1783, hydrogen was found in water. Also when Uranus was in Cancer from 1866-72 Mendel set out the laws of heredity and founded genetics. Just as, when Uranus last crossed Cancer in 1949-56, the structure of DNA was discovered and we also had the advent of contraception with the 'pill' changing women's lives. An overview of these zodiacal journeys features in the 'Uranus-Neptune-Pluto' edition of the *Éditions Traditionnelles*.

Naturally it's appropriate to analyse the charts of the configurations in order to understand them better, especially these 'universal constitutions', as the ancients called them, that are the conjunctions. Likewise we need to note the repeated patterns that install a certain climate. Thus, in 1939, I looked into the role of Saturn which was near the MC in the birth charts of Hitler, Goering and Himmler, and also when the Nazis took power in Germany,[4] with the same thing happening at the ingress in the spring and summer of 1939, as with the lunation at the outbreak of war.

Now, computerized astro-cartography gives us the signs[5] where the planets cross the meridian and the horizon on the terrestial planisphere so that we can locate the position of historical events. This is a marvellous tool as long as we don't rush to make predictions. For example, when looking at the chart of the United States and that of the war in 1941 would we be happy to give significance to Pluto being on the MC of Hiroshima, when no angular line crosses Calvados, or France even, to mark the impact of the colossal and decisive attack that followed the Allied landings in Normandy in 1945? It's true that my investigations into about sixty outbreaks of war and ceasefires have put an end to the widely held belief that firstly Mars and secondly Venus or Jupiter are always found on the horizon or the meridian of the world charts. Things are not that simple, so it's going to be a headache for the person improvising as they survey their linear maps.

Ultimately, the prevailing dynamic when we feel we are getting nowhere is with the pendulum-like, binary rhythm of the cycle and it is this that has the last word: flux-reflux, increase-decrease, rise-fall, Eros-Thanatos..., this being the heart of the general configuration of the solar system.

War or revolution?
Many sociologists consider wars and revolutions as the interchangeable ills of societies in crisis. So any evaluation of the danger of war depends on the circumstances at the time

and both war and revolution are a possibility. The concept of an ominous configuration having an 'active principle' that gives it the power to create a crisis with heightened potential lets us know that the kind of dangerous times that we associate with war or revolution are coming but we don't know any more.

When we look at history it is evident that there are many possibilities: the Jupiter-Uranus conjunction 'gave' us the glorious French Revolution of 1789 (positive for the most part but ending so badly) and the Saturn-Pluto conjunction the terrible war of 1914.

Also, a slow planet can intervene when it passes over the location of a previous grand conjunction and awakens its potential. Thus the campaign conducted by Nazi Germany against Bolshevism and the spirit of the French Revolution was able to proceed when Pluto transited the zodiacal position of the Saturn-Neptune conjunction in 1917 and the Jupiter-Uranus conjunction of 1789. Likewise, the Jupiter-Uranus conjunction of 1983 happened at the position of the Saturn-Neptune conjunction of 1809, correlating with the South American revolution, the rebellion of the Latin American colonies around 1810 (Venezuela, Argentina, Chile, Mexico, Colombia, Paraguay, Bolivia, Peru, Uruguay, Ecuador). However, even if these countries had gained their independence this continent would still have been subject to the economic of *'made in the US'*.

This was how I came to make the forecast in my article entitled 'The Jupiter-Uranus conjunction of 1983' published in *'L'astrologue* no. 60 in the 4th trimester of 1982.

> It's quite interesting that the Saturn-Neptune conjunction of 1809 at 6° of Sagittarius is at the opposition of the 1775 Jupiter-Uranus conjunction at 3° of Gemini, at the time of the American War of
> Independence, and our conjunction of 1983 is going to be formed at the same position as the first and opposite that of the second. One wonders if a revolutionary movement concerning the Latin American continent could lead to its economic and political emancipation from the US.

Yet, according to most economists and historians at the time such a forecast was highly improbable. They saw Latin-America as being like a sick society that would remain mired in a vicious circle that condemned the future to be the same as the past. It was nonetheless at this turning point that general emancipation of Latin America began and led to them achieving full autonomous prosperity before the end of the century.

From revolution to economic chaos
'Suddenly society finds itself reduced to a temporary state of barbarism: it's as if there was a famine or a devastating war and the means of existence was cut off...' Set down by Marx and Engels in their Communist Party Manifesto, this picture of an economic depression at its worst hardly seems exaggerated to economists today, because society as a whole is ruined. It's the equivalent of a bloodbath in war or the devastation caused by revolutions. This then is a third variation.

Thus, essentially, economic revolutions in society, at least in the West, are linked to a trio which combines the cycles of Jupiter and Saturn with that of Uranus, with the Uranus-Neptune cycle as the framework. The relationship between the aspects of the planetary trio in question and the economy was long ago observed by Brahe in Belgium and, from 1932, by Langham in the US. The improvement here is that we have a better overview. Here is a graph of the cyclic indicator relative to the interference of Jupiter-Saturn-Uranus for the 19th and 20th centuries. Covering two centuries it is crossed by two Saturn-Uranus cycles, intertwined with the Jupiter-Uranus cycle with its peaks (oppositions) and troughs (conjunctions) which happen every seven years. We have to do our best to decipher the pattern.

Professional economic forecasters are aware of the importance of cycles in the recurrence and duration of boom and bust. There have been times when they forgot about them as, for example, after the Second World War when we had thirty consecutive years of growth (except for 1965 when the economy overheated, exactly at the time of the Saturn-Uranus opposition). The constant annual growth of 5% doubled the standard of living in one generation and was an exceptional boost to morale. As a resul, a futurologist like Hermann Kahn could become famous for his optimistic curved lines drawn in the image of his opulent personage.

With the return of crisis, the value of cycles was again brought to mind with Kondratiev making a major comeback. Before the war he had discovered a great economic cycle with two phases that alternated between rises and falls which affected prices, production and employment.

There is, however, a connection between the rhythm of this cycle and that of the Saturn-Uranus cycle. Thus, according to the author, three long phases of economic expansion are observable: from 1848-50 to 1872-73, from 1896 to 1920, then from 1940-45 to 1974. These alternated with three other long inverse phases of economic downturn: from 1817 to 1848, from 1873 to 1896 and from 1920 to the Second World War. This exactly mirrors the alternating ascendant and descendant phases of the Saturn-Uranus cycle with its successive conjunctions and oppositions.

See diagrams on opposite page and overleaf.

The Jupiter-Uranus Cycle

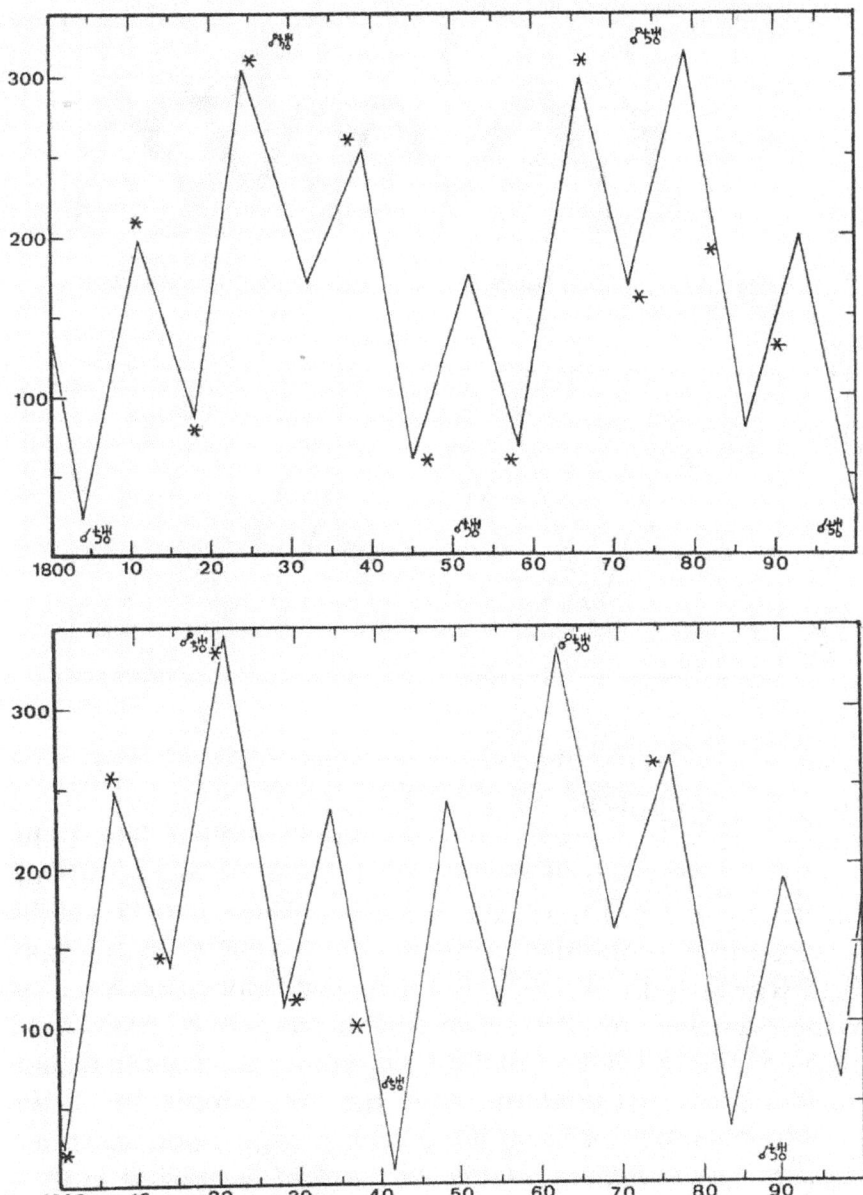

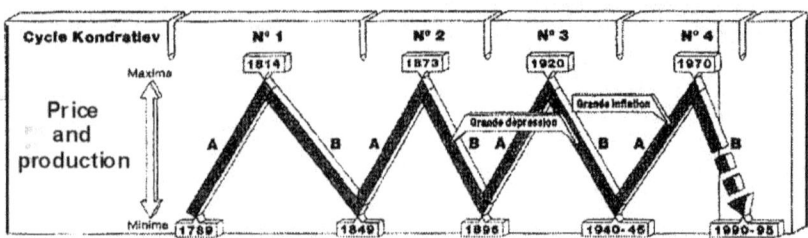

Extract from *Un dossier de l'Expansion : Deux siècles de révolution industrielle* (Pluriel; 1983).

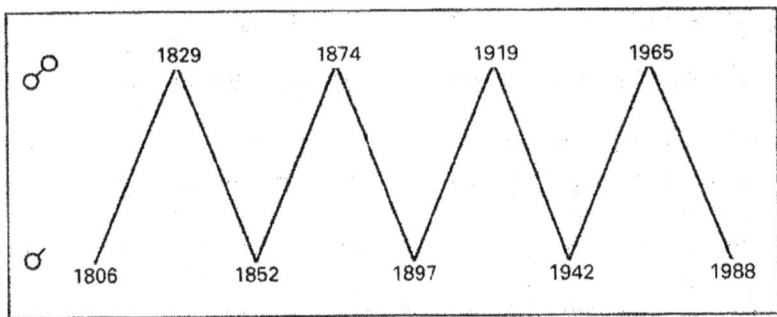

Thus you have the successive conjunctions of 1852, 1897 and 1942 and the oppositions of 1874 and 1919. Five out of the seven observed pivotal points completely tallied. The only discrepancy was with the two others. Thus the opposition of 1829 diverged from the peak in the economy in 1817, while the ascending economic curve which started with the last world war lasted until 1974, with the last opposition already having occurred in 1965. However, in the case of 1965 there was a change at the end of 1964 when a mini-crisis that had occurred previously put an end to the expansionist fever. '*In our view, there was no more glory after 1965, the year when we started to reject children, started to reject life*' asserted Alfred Sauvy in 'L'Expansion' no. 200.

Naturally the cycle is influenced by the interference of other cycles, just as the economy is not strictly the prisoner of a mechanistic straitjacket. The justification for Kondratiev's cycle is that it is based on the fluctuations associated with inventions and creations with advances in technology contributing to an explosion in productivity. There were precisely two energetic periods of creativity around the time of the conjunctions of 1852 and of 1897, which were based on two industrial revolutions, the first of coal and steel, the second of oil and electricity. As for the creative stimulus accompanying the last Saturn-Uranus conjunction in 1992, that stemmed from the revolution in information technology, with the arrival of the Internet following on the sudden appearance of the mobile phone and all the panoply of electronic innovations which have transformed society.

The Saturn-Uranus cycle is also influenced by the relentless Jupiter-Uranus cycle with its lesser rhythm of seven years, and this also has an effect on the general distribution of economic crises: 1810, 1818, 1825, 1837, 1847, 1857, 1866, 1873, 1882, 1890, 1900, 1907, 1913, 1920, 1929, 1937, 1974... Out of the seventeen crises in question, it's remarkable that fourteen occurred at crucial periods or when the cycle was changing direction; six times the aspect was formed in the same year and for the rest it was formed within one year to eighteen months.

I am not familiar with the practice of market or economic forecasting and I doubt if this initial evaluation would be sufficient. Nevertheless, it would be a good idea when undertaking such an enterprise to begin with just such an exploration of the cycles.

Chapter 4 - The Jupiter-Neptune Cycle

The Jupiter-Neptune conjunction occurs about every 13 years, usually moving forward from one sign to the next, and its passage through the 20th century stretched from Cancer in 1906 to Capricorn in 1984 and 1997 and Aquarius in 2009.[6]

Generally humid, temperate and diffuse, the 'active principle' emphasizes the Neptunian current of unified collective global power. Here the huge, elastic, moderating, generous Jupiterian mode aims for unity and peaceful exchange; in brief, it is humanitarian. There is a general atmosphere of diplomatic and political détente and collective movements that have liberal democratic tendencies. In effect, its ideology is socialist, a beneficial power which favours universal moral values.

Here is a list of events observed at the cyclic leaps starting at the end of the 18th century:

<u>1792 in Libra</u>: The First French Republic.

<u>1804 in Scorpio</u>: The end of this Republic. The First Empire which followed it (Uranian conjunctions of 1803 and 1805) took the liberal spirit of the French Revolution to the continent.

<u>1818 in Sagittarius</u>: Alarmed by reactionary politics of the Holy Alliance, the liberal movement gained momentum.

<u>1830 in Capricorn</u> (with a Jupiter-Uranus conjunction): the revolutionary European movement of 1830 (France, Belgium, Poland, Germany, Italy). The first liberal victories: Greek and Belgian independence. France and England empowered a new social class, the bourgeoisie, while, on their side of the Atlantic, the United States became a democracy.

<u>1843 in Aquarius</u>: Chartist agitation in England in 1842; the first general strikes affected half the country and trade unions took off the following year. The 'Franco-German Annals' founded in 1843 was a network of clandestine revolutionary minds which found success in Bohemia and

Poland. The same year the Risorgimento stepped aside in favour of Italian unity. Preparations for a Franco-English entente cordiale were already underway. The first rumblings were heard which presaged the explosion in 1848 when the next Saturn-Neptune conjunction provided a revolutionary climate.

1856 in Pisces: This year, in Germany, the bourgeoisie revived the Zollverein, its political implementation propelled by economic agitation. It was the same in Russia when Alexander II opened the frontiers and the prisons, opening the way for liberal evolution. But above all this was the year of the Treaty of Paris, a victory for Franco-British liberalism which settled various European problems such as the Black Sea, the Danube and the Ottoman Empire as well as laying the foundations of international maritime law.

1869 in Aries: A successful year for Gambetta's Republican Party which, the following year, helped France change its Liberal Empire to the Third Republic. In England a liberal majority with a radical bent in 1868 was followed by electoral reforms in Scotland and Ireland. On the German side, the first signs of social democracy with the creation of the Social Democrat party of Bebel and Liebknecht. In 1868 there was the Japanese revolution, the Serbian constitution and the opening of the Suez Canal and the following year trade unions appeared in America.

1881 in Taurus: Creation of a European entente in 1881-82: The Triple Alliance of Germany, Austria and Italy was supported by Romania and Serbia, and partially by Greece, Turkey, Spain and Sweden. These two years saw the development of legislation in Germany and France which allowed press freedom, the right of assembly and, importantly, introduced free primary education, which, under the Third French Republic, was secular and compulsory.

1894 in Gemini: In France there was the first strong socialist push at the elections of 1893, with forty deputies elected under the banner of Jean Jaures, and the birth of the General

Confederation of Labour in 1895. In Russia, at the beginning of the year, Lenin founded the League of Struggle for the Emancipation of the Working Class.

1907 in Cancer: Triple Entente England-France-Italy. In the space of three years the Liberal Party[7] with the support of Ramsey MacDonald's Labour Party voted in a series of labour laws. In France the radicals and socialists were successful in the 1906 elections, the General Confederation of Labour held a number of strikes. A revolutionary climate spread throughout Europe: Austria-Hungary, Russia, Spain. The United States also took a democratic turn in 1906 and equally the following year there was a peace conference at The Hague.

1919-20 in Leo: End of the First World War with victory for the Allies (11 November 11 1918), followed by the Treaty of Versailles and the founding of the League of Nations and the creation of the Third International.

1932 in Virgo: Under the aegis of the League of Nations, the disarmament conference in Geneva ended in a failure for collective security (Neptune in fall and Jupiter in detriment). The Four-Power-Pact in Rome took over the reins with their diplomatic efforts strengthened by the support of the Soviet Union, won over at last to the cause of the democracies against fascism (1932-33). The Spanish Republic of 1931. In November 1932, a victory for the Democrats in the United States put F. D. Roosevelt in the White House.

1945 in Libra: End of the Second World War with victory for the Allies (May and August 1945) and the founding of the United Nations (UN) in June 1945: Straight after the war the tide turned in favour of the left and those who had resisted: there was a Labour government in England and the IVth Republic in France. On 12 April 1945 Roosevelt died. He had been re-elected many times and he held the American presidency for the whole of the 1932-45 cycle.

1958 in Scorpio: De Gaulle having returned to power in France, the Fourth Republic became the Fifth (October 1958).

There was a revolution in Cuba with Fidel Castro becoming Prime Minister (January 1959). Also an American-Soviet détente, with nuclear tests suspended on both sides in March 1958, and the following year Vice president Nixon visited Moscow and Khrushchev visited the United States.

1971 in Sagittarius: This conjunction, which lasted the whole of 1971, saw a turning point in general East-West relations. Chancellor Willy Brandt brought about Ostpolitik which improved relations with the communist bloc. The groundwork had already been done by the German-Soviet pact (August 1970), which widened to the German-Polish pact in November 1970, and finally the quadripartite accord in Berlin in September 1971. This climate of détente warmed the negotiations between the two great powers and the SALT 1 treaty limiting their strategic weapons was signed in May 1972. Furthermore, there was also detente in Asia. In August 1971, Sino-American contact ended with Communist China being admitted to the UN in October 1971, and in February 1972 there was President Nixon's trip to Peking. Very like the preceding conjunction when Castro seized power in Cuba, at this one, on 24 October 1970, Salvador Allende came to power in Chile, sadly not for long. In 1971, Bernard Kouchner founded Médecins sans frontières and Greenpeace also was founded this year, during the following cycle, the first environmental organization in the world.   1984 in Capricorn: The road to peace. On the edge of an abyss with Euro missiles head to head in Europe and the climate of 'star wars', the two superpowers were forced, in extremis, to negotiate. Chernenko agreed to more arms control talks on 20 May 1984, but more importantly, as the Sun approached the separating conjunction (22 December 1984), Mikhail Gorbachev, with his Sun-Jupiter trine, took over the reins of power. Negotiations between the new Soviet number one and President Reagan lead to peac, and in April 1984, relations between the US and Communist China were regularized. Furthermore, the trend towards democracy flowing through Latin America manifested in Argentina, Uruguay and Brazil in 1983-85. In France, in the government of the Fifth Republic, Laurent Fabius, on the left, took over from Pierre Maurois.

1997 in Aquarius: A special conjunction because reinforced by a Jupiter-Uranus conjunction, the trio Jupiter-Neptune-Uranus being within an 8° span. This corresponded with a United Nations Convention about climate change held in Kyoto in December 1997 with the aim of getting a better hold on societies across the world. In Europe, after the rigid Thatcherite era, the United Kingdom had Tony Blair's New Labour, Lionel Jospin was socializing France and the Social Democrat Gerhard Schröder was in Germany.
2009 in Aquarius: An American presidential election installed an Afro-American, Barack Obama, in the White House for the first time. More humane than his opponents who were too fond of their purses, he was deservedly returned to power in November 2012.[8]

The last eighteen Jupiter-Neptune conjunctions in a row form a continuum with phenomena, which are undeniably of same order, being repeated every thirteen years: the beginning, end or renewal of a historical process with the same tendency which is of a collective liberal order, democratic, socialist or even more or less revolutionary. There is a swing to the left, with international aims of an associative, peaceful or humanitarian nature. If the Jupiter-Uranus conjunction calls to mind 1914 and 1941, it also brought us to 1918 and 1945.

Throughout the cycle, there is a sequence of events. History unfolds itself starting at one conjunction and ending at the next. The First French Republic, the League of Nations, the Roosevelt experience, the Fourth French Republic: all within the life of one cycle. Alternatively, a trend that starts at one conjunction may continue through many cycles: the European liberal movement which took shape in 1817, came to power in 1830 and then became dominant at the time of the Entente Cordiale in 1843. The political debut of Lenin in 1894 was established at the first Russian Revolution of 1907. And then there were the great armistices of 1918 and 1945, as

The Jupiter-Neptune Cycle

well as the great international conferences: The Hague in 1907, League of Nations in 1919, the failed peace in 1932, the United Nations in 1945, general détente in 1971, then in 1984, with the Kyoto Convention of 1997.

The creation of time periods using the high points belonging to the same cyclic family invites us to attach historical relationships to the bounds of the successive conjunctions, but within each cycle Ariadne's thread has to be woven from one aspect to the next, making the parts a continuous whole all the way from one end to the other.

Cycle 1918-32: The League of Nations

Conjunction (September 1919), 10° Leo: Birth. With the encouragement of President Wilson, the League of Nations (LN) was founded at the Versailles Peace Conference on 10 January 1920. Its mission was peace. It was an unprecedented experiment in collective security; the first to bring together most of the countries in the world.

Sextile (December 1921-August 1922): The Washington conference on disarmament opened on October 28 1921. All the great powers were there and agreed on the limitation naval armaments and also settled problems in the Far East; a first step along the road to collective security.

Square (January-October 1923): The Corfu incident. A confrontation between Italy and Greece: in August 1923 Corfu was bombarded and occupied by Italian troops. Mussolini, not recognizing League of Nations jurisdiction, wanted to settle this problem himself. Mustapha Kemal, the Turkish leader, rejected the Treaty of Sèvres but agreed to the Treaty of Lausanne on 23 July.

Trine (March-November 1924): The Geneva Protocol. Both the English and French heads of state inaugurated the Geneva Assembly, making it an instrument of European renewal. Amidst great hopes the League of Nations became a political reality and Geneva became the centre of international life. On 1 October 1924 the representatives of forty-seven nations signed the Geneva Protocol condemning all recourse to war and asserting the principle of compulsory arbitration before the permanent Court of International Justice. They agreed that it was necessary to impose sanctions on states which refused this arbitration.

Opposition (April-December 1926): Germany joins the League of Nations. The Assembly of 8 September 1926 agreed to the admission of Germany to Geneva (it had been excluded). Thus the Reich entered the League of Nations, a natural evolution, though this change involved a reconsideration of the enemy and an effort at reintegration. Coexistence of opposites: this about-turn was what eventually caused the decline of the Geneva institutions.

Trine (May-December 1928): The Paris Pact. The democracies pronounced war to be unlawful! Sixty nations made a solemn commitment to not resort to the use of arms to impose their policies. The illustrious Kellogg-Briand pact was signed in Paris on 27 August 1928. It covered all of Europe (except for the USSR) and Africa and even parts of America. The League of Nations was at the height of its prestige, seen as the 'Parliament of the World', besides which a declaration like this heightened the belief that a universal durable peace was possible.

Square (June 1929-January 1930): Failure of the federal project. In September 1929, Briand put forward the idea that European powers should unite and, in May 1930, went as far as publishing a program for European federal union. The project was not well received.

Sextile (July 1930): Towards disarmament. In the summer of 1930 the commission preparing for the disarmament conference published a draft for a convention.

Conjunction (September 1932) in Virgo, both planets in detriment in this sign: the project for collective security was a failure. Seventy-two nations attended the disarmament conference which opened on the 2 February 1932. The conference was a failure and, on 27 March 1933, Japan gave notice that it was leaving the League of Nations; Nazi Germany followed suit on 21 October dashing the League's hopes of collective security.

Cycle 1932-45 from the collapse of the League of Nations to the birth of the United Nations

Conjunction (September 1932): Genevan revival. A diplomatic bombshell: as Japan and Germany withdrew, the Soviet Union, hitherto neutral, filled the gap. In 1932 the USSR, whose previous enemies had been the agents of the Quai d'Orsay and intelligence services working for western capitalism, now made Hitler their number one enemy: thus the Soviet Union joined the western democracies and their drive for collective security. The Kremlin gave a new impetus to French diplomacy and Paris and Moscow were now together in the fight against Germany.

Semi-square (October 1934): The assassination of the French Foreign Minister Louis Barthou who was the main architect of the policy of European unity against Hitler. On 9 October 1934 Barthou met his death when King Alexander of Yugoslavia was assassinated. Also, Germany demanded the rearmament that it had asked for in the spring.

Sextile (December 1934-July 1935): The USSR at Geneva and the Stresa Front. On 18 September 1934 the Soviets were admitted to Geneva and became the principal partner in the League of Nations. Their membership initiated a new era and revitalized collective security. As the Third Reich became more threatening, cooperation was strengthened by the formation of a front at the Stresa Conference (11-14 April 1935). There was a Franco-Italian accord 7 January 1935, a Franco- Soviet pact 2 May, a Soviet-Czechoslovak treaty 16 May. Britain also engaged in diplomatic efforts in February.

Square (January-September 1936): Collective failure. Under a Saturn-Neptune opposition squared by Jupiter, 1936 saw the crises multiply: the occupation of the Rhineland, the Italo-Ethiopian war, the Sino-Japanese war and the war in Spain. And after the LN imposed ineffectual sanctions on Italy it fell into the arms of Germany. Thus the Stresa Front was shattered and on 1 November 1936 came the proclamation of a Rome-Berlin axis.

Trine (February October 1937): Appeasement: 1937 brought a brief respite to a Europe in turmoil. There was no chance of any improvement but at least there were some positive elements: an Anglo-Italian agreement over the status quo in the Mediterranean, a Franco-Yugoslavian accord and, above all, France and Britain became closer with their gentleman's agreement at the beginning of 1938. But the quincunx was not far off with the storm over Munich.

Opposition (April 1939): The Soviet volte-face and war. Moscow, excluded from the sinister 'four power pact' signed in Munich, became alienated by the ambiguous diplomacy of London and Paris. The turnaround began in March and concluded in August. It took place, when the cycle had gone 180° from conjunction to opposition. Having lost faith in the democratic camp, the USSR signed the German-Soviet pact. Soon after, the Second World War started. At the following Jupiter-Neptune conjunction, these partners would again be united at the victorious conclusion of the war.

Trine (May 1941): The Atlantic Charter. In the absence of an international body, solidarity was achieved by the democracies in the war cooperating with each other and the United States took over the reins. The democrat President F. D. Roosevelt had been in the White House since the conjunction of 1932. At the time of the previous opposition the United States had been in isolation, having signed the Neutrality Act of 5 September 1939. Now that was about to change when, with the Lend-Lease Act of 11 March 1941, the US became an arsenal providing military supplies to the allies. Furthermore, on 14 August 1941 the Atlantic Charter, the basis of the new economic and political cooperation between the democratic states, was signed by Roosevelt and Churchill. Moreover, in September 1941 a tripartite conference was held in Moscow which focussed on the assistance that America and Britain could give the USSR, which was under German attack.

Square (May 1942): The US enters the war: On 7 December 1941 the Japanese attack on Pearl Harbour precipitated the American entry into the war and initially they suffered a number of defeats.

Sextile (June 1943): First victories. In 1943 the Allied armies, having been on the losing side went on the offensive. In November 1942 the Allies landed in North Africa, a prelude to the attack on 'fortress Europe'.

Conjunction (September 1945) in Libra: The armistice, the Allied victory and the United Nations. On 8 May 1945 Nazi Germany capitulated, followed by Japan on 2 September. Roosevelt died on April 2 and was succeeded by Harry Truman. The war over, the US joined the other countries in founding and organising a new international body for collective security, the United Nations.

In going round the cycle, we have met with the times most notable for bringing order to humanity.

The following conjunction of 1958, at the beginning of Scorpio, was not expressed in this way being still too near to the post-war set-up of a world divided into two opposing camps. On the other hand in 1971, the year of the following conjunction in the early degrees of Sagittarius, there was a veritable feast of diplomacy: Britain admitted into the Common Market, Nixon's surprise visit to Peking which triggered a Sino-American thaw, the meeting of Brandt and Brezhnev, China joining the UN, Kosygin's round-trips, Brezhnev's visits to France and Tito's to the US. But above all, after ten months of negotiations and twenty-one meetings, the European Conference delivered the German-Soviet and German-Polish treaties. This was a major turning point. Then there was the Berlin Agreement of 3 September 1971 when, after seventeen months and thirty-three negotiating sessions, the four great powers (US-USSR-Great Britain- France) turned the page on twenty-five years of European post-war history.

At the following conjunction of 1984, we were rescued *in extremis* from the new hell of a menacing Jupiter-Uranus conjunction. Since May 1983 our continent had been on the edge of a nuclear precipice with the siting of Pershing missiles and SS 20's on either side of the Iron Curtain. The radical transition from tension to détente began with an international conference in Stockholm in January 1984. There was a lasting thaw after January 1985, when the effort that was put into the peace process grew throughout the cycle. At the trine of 1987-88 the Reagan-Gorbachev negotiations ended with the dismantling of nuclear arms, and before the end of the century the two great powers had become friends. The opposition September 1989–June 1990), was the epilogue with the last negotiations and the Soviet Union on the way to extinction. This opposition was part of a rarely seen configuration in which Jupiter opposed a triple Saturn-Uranus-Neptune conjunction: a sweep of the brush affecting millions of people across the world and a crucial watershed which I forecasted at the previous conjunction in 1953.

After this upheaval, the following conjunction of 1997 seems to have brought some respite but, conversely, at the opposition (September 2002-June 2003) there were public demonstrations against the Anglo-America intervention in Iraq. The collective fever brought the whole world on to the streets. On 15 February 2003, ten million people in Europe marched against their governments who had miserably aligned themselves with the warmongering of George W. Bush and the apprentice sorcerers of the Pentagon. Five million were still marching at the end of the following week and they were still marching at the end of the month in Asia and America! The UN, which was implicated (at the previous opposition) in the First Iraq War, this time was truly flouted, and had this second war imposed on it unbeknownst. When it comes down to it, as well as being a complete disaster, this was an illegal war (they didn't find any trace of 'weapons of mass destruction, nor of connivance between Bin Laden and Saddam Hussein'). Then, in an atmosphere of general discord, at the last conjunction in 2010, American voters, in line with the humanitarian nature of this configuration, elected a Afro-American man to the White House for the first time—Barack Obama.

Chapter 5 – The Jupiter-Pluto Cycle

Of the ten or so great planetary cycles, this is the one that unites the swiftest planet with the slowest with an average duration of 12.5 years over the course of the 20th century. The line-up of conjunctions is as follows; 1906, 1918, 1931, 1943, 1956, 1968, 1981 and 1994, and they went from Gemini through to Scorpio.

The best way to understand how this cycle operates is to look at a configuration which places the phenomenon in a position of maximum dissonance. The conjunction of 1931, for example, was at the centre of an exceptionally discordant arena which involved all the outer planets. In this case this Jupiter-Pluto hybrid was opposed by Saturn and square to Uranus as well as being semi-square to Neptune, the five planets having come together to produce ten dissonances in all.

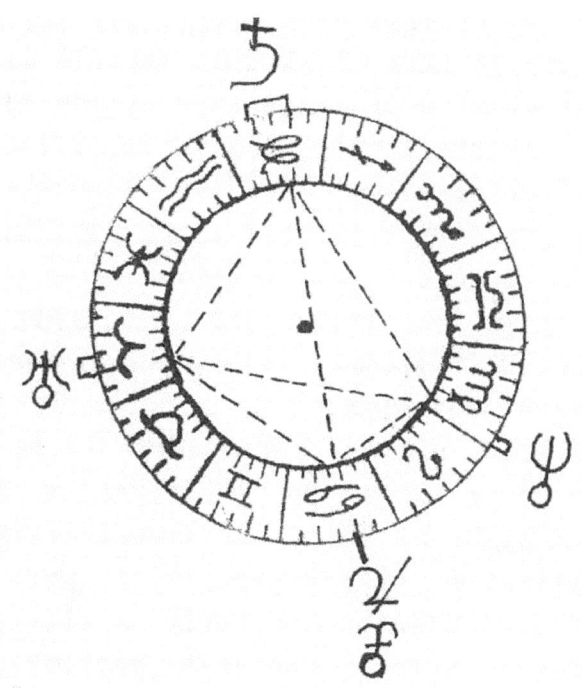

It's not surprising that this rare phenomenon fell in a handful of the most critical years in the 20th century. Remember the great world economic crisis which erupted on 24 October 1929 and which was in full swing in 1932: the collapse of industrial production and the worst unemployment figures.

Cycle 1918-31
It all began with the <u>conjunction</u> of 1918. What started then was born out of the suffering caused by losing the war and the iniquitous peace treaty with its disastrous consequences. Adolf Hitler's political career started the following year (the conjunction had a 2° orb for the first quarter of 1919). On 12 September , charged by a section of military intelligence to monitor a small German workers party, he joined the fledgling small group of a few hundred members and discovered his talent as an orator. At the sextile, in July 1921, he became head of the party that he had already shaped (swastika, brown shirts...) and gathered the party's first team around him: Hess, Rosenberg, Röhm, Streicher, and shortly after, Himmler, Goering, then Goebbels. This was to become the 'party of the Führer'.

At the outgoing <u>trine</u>, the occupation of the Ruhr by the French army in January 1923 was a harmful intervention made worse by the national furore it caused: the currency collapsed and there was dire poverty...The Nazi movement now had more than 50,000 members and its reach extended to individuals like Ludendorff. At the sesqui-quadrate there was the failed Munich putsch of 8 November 1923: there was a trial and a thirteen-month prison sentence.

At the perfection of the <u>opposition</u> in 1925, despite the success of *Mein Kampf*, Hitler's prestigious companion in arms Ludendorff distanced himself and the party went into crisis. In years to come Hitler was to blame Ludendorff for the party's sharp decline. Hitler was no longer a danger and at the elections to the Reichstag on 20 May 1928 his party only received 2.6% of the vote and won only twelve seats. Unusually it was at the square, followed by the sextile, that he gained the capitalist backing of Hugenberg, patron of Krupp and press magnate, and Baron Von Papen who helped him get his foot on the ladder.

Cycle 1931-43
When the great economic crisis brought Germany to the brink (the closure of the banks on13 July 1931, etc.), there was an unexpected Nazi surge which reached its height in 1932. At the new conjunction Hitler was at the gates of power. The ultimate promotion: on 13 March 1932 he stood in the presidential election against President Hindenburg and beat him in the second round obtaining 37% of the 13 million votes. The following 31 July he had enough of a voice to merit 230 seats in the Reichstag. They were now the majority party with Goering as their president.

At the sextile, on 30 January 1933, a little after midday under a dissonant Sun-Mercury-Saturn conjunction on the MC, he is now Chancellor of the Reich about to plunge the world into darkness during his twelve years in power. His demented regime immediately established the first concentration camp in Dachau, book burning and a fanatical cult chanting 'Heil Hitler' with arm outstretched while ruffians in jack boots did the goose step.

The great purge, on 30 June 1934, known as 'the night of the long knives' happened at the square: the assassination of the section chiefs of the storm troopers and others (83 dead!): the victims were the party's unruly army directed by Ernst Röhm, Hitler's untamed military right arm. Apart from this, on July 25 following (Sun conjunct Pluto), there was the failed SS putsch in Austria with the assassination of President Dollfuss.

At the trine of 1935 there was the vote, on 13 January, that returned the Saar to Germany, followed by a tour de force on 16 March when Hitler created a new Wehrmacht of 36 divisions with obligatory military service. Also an Anglo-German naval accord on 18 June undermined the Stresa Front that had been agreed by the League.

On 7 March 1936, the year of the quincunx, Hitler got one over the European community by seizing the Rhineland without encountering any opposition. On 11 July 11 he formed the Rome-Berlin axis and enlarged it at the end of the year by establishing the Anti-Comintern Pact with Japan.

The opposition hovered over all of 1937 when the 'Lebensraum policy', an ideology proposing German expansion, was seized on in a Hitlerian frenzy. Now nothing could stop this dictator who already had a hand in the war in Spain (Guernica 26 April). He was in control of the Wehrmacht and had the hawkish Ribbentrop as Foreign Minister. Thus he embarked on his numerous conquests: first Austria, then Czechoslovakia, then Poland.

You can see the connection between the trine of 1939 and the German-Soviet pact because it breaks down at the square of 1940: the consequence of Molotov's visit to Berlin in November 1939.

By the same token, it's natural to link the approaching sextile of June 1941 and the following semi-square in September, to the turnaround in the German-Soviet war. It was glorious at first, as General Halder, the land army's chief of staff and second in command to Hitler wrote in his notebook: *'The Russian campaign has been won in the space of two weeks'* (July 3). This was understandable, considering the rapid advance of the Wehrmacht into great stretches of Russian territory, with thousands of enemy planes destroyed, hundreds of thousands of prisoners and the Red Army giving the impression of having already been defeated. But later he wrote: *'It's more and mor clear that we have underestimated the Russian colossus'* (11 August). The terrible realization and a deep sense of foreboding which, for Hitler, manifested as a severe attack of dysentery during the first week of August (as the Sun transited his Saturn). And above all, while the sextile had been fleeting; the semi-square dragged on until the spring of 1942!

What followed was a decisive turning point in the war which came at the conjunction of 1943, with the overthrow of Mussolini in Italy on 23 July, then the irreparable defeat at

Stalingrad (February 2 1943) at the same time as that of Rommel's Africa Korps: the Nazi tide now begins to ebb and the retreat now underway will end in the rubble of Berlin.

From the end of 1942 to mid-1943, Jupiter returned to the positions it had occupied in 1919, when Hitler's political ideas emerged, and in 1931 when, like a sea of black, the swastika was planted at the portals of power. Now, in 1943, the lugubrious Nazi adventure was ending in apocalypse. Two years later, at the time of the Jupiter-Neptune conjunction, the war ended. Hitler had been in power less than twelve years, from the sextile of 1933 to the semi-square of 1945, but his hold on power had already been weakened at the conjunction of 1943, the year when the Allies were winning on all fronts.

We now will leave this monstrous barbarism, the repertoire of Pluto's negative qualities being assimilated into the savagery of a primitive return to chaos. However, sometimes something great rises out of the depths. Let's return to the series of conjunctions in the previous century to get an overview.

The first one in 1906 gives us an idea. This was the year when someone special who was then unknown, a certain Gandhi, who was born under the conjunction of 1869, started a campaign of boycotts in South Africa because the rights of the poor and oppressed were not being respected. Also that year, Indian nationalists came together for the first time to call for independence. The demands were reiterated with a vengeance at the following conjunction after an unarmed crowd was savagely attacked by a British general (379 dead and 1200 wounded!) on 13 April 1919 at Amritsar in the Punjab. Gandhi then embarked on a successful campaign of non-cooperation and civil disobedience. At the following conjunction of 1931 at the London conference on India his role as the liberator of his country was confirmed. Then close to the following conjunction in 1942, having taken over from Nehru, he called on a more aggressive congress to end all negotiations with Great Britain and to encourage the protest movement: 'British out of India' together with the full resumption of non-violent resistance. Although the nationalist leaders were still in prison, they already knew, because of the war going on outside, that the game was won. This story demonstrates the power of disobedience, the Plutonian word being here the victory of the word 'no' in order that good can prevail.

Apart from the conjunction of 1918-19 in Cancer being about the power of death, it also marks the passing of the great families who had ruled the continent: after the Romanovs, who were eliminated when Pluto entered the sign, there was the Hohenzollern family, the Habsburgs and other princes in Baden, Bavaria, Württemberg.

In returning to the abyss of the anal complex with the appeal of all things dirty, ugly, bad or evil, it seems pertinent to mention the devastating consequences of Prohibition in the United States around the time of the conjunction of 1931: the clandestine trafficking of alcohol which resulted in the corruption which poisoned the state institutions and gave rise to gangsterism, the criminalization of state power, and prostitution in this great country: a corruption which was to plague the western world.

At the following conjunction of 1943 in Leo we saw the ultimate drive towards death. A real explosion of the Plutonian power of Thanatos: on 15 March 1943, Oppenheimer was commissioned to build an atomic bomb. The bomb contained plutonium and it exploded under the solar and lunar conjunctions with Pluto, which was semi-square to Jupiter, on 6 and 9 August 1945 over Hiroshima and Nagasaki.

A new rebellion by the poor: from 17 to 24 April 1955, just before the conjunction of November 1955 to June 1956, twenty-nine newly independent countries in Asia and Africa came together for the first time for a conference in the Indonesian town of Bandung: it gave birth to a neutralist Third World movement that condemned colonialism and racial segregation and the cause was national liberation. In 1955, Afro-Americans, with pastor Martin Luther King, achieved their first victory in 1956 when segregation was banned on urban transport. The same year also saw the insurrections in Poland and Hungary while Africa, Morocco and Tunisia gained their independence and Algeria was still fighting for its own. It was the time of rock, the music, with its liberating effect on morals, extolled by white singers.

At the next stage of the cycle, it is difficult to differentiate between the Jupiter-Uranus conjunction and the Jupiter-Pluto conjunction alongside it, this last having taken place in October 1968 in Virgo while the first lasted from the end of 1968 to mid-1969 in Libra. At this time there was a real explosion of youth culture around the world which brought about a wild release of tension, with the old demons belonging to a sulphurous Pluto coming out of the closet. Certainly and very much positively, in the climate of Neptune in Scorpio, the sexual revolution imposed on society (contraception, free abortion) had a belated liberating effect on women, but equally it was infinitely devastating for a youth that was immature to be presented with unbridled eroticism, and then there were the drugs that made a sudden and devastating appearance across the world.

Furthermore, just as Hungary had submitted to a communist dictatorship at the previous conjunction, Czechoslovakia now had to suffer the same fate. Also, Colonel Gaddafi, who came to power after a revolution in Libya, became the source of Arab state terrorism with devastating affect internationally. With Pluto in Virgo, black polluting oil slicks contaminated the world and there was the sudden realization that an endangered nature was being destroyed and had to be saved by ecology. In another expression of Virgo; an oppressed minority was given support: in Egypt on 3 February 1969 the PLO. and its president Yasser Arafat were recognized by Arab nations.

The conjunction of 2 September 2 1981 at 24° Libra came close on the conference in Cancun, Mexico (21 to 23 October), which was tasked with restarting the North-South dialogue so that more support could be given to developing countries, formerly known as the Third World. The confrontation between North and South, known as the Falklands War was not included. A new rebellion: a dissident movement started in Poland with Solidarity, a union set up to undermine the power of the government. Jaruzelski declared a 'state of war' in the country. Jupiter does not in any way divest Pluto of its power to awaken the primitive survival instincts of cavemen, the savagery that causes the depths of human misery. Thus, with the aid of Iran's ayatollahs, 1981 saw the rise of a fanatical Islamic jihad which confronted the religious fanaticism of Israel in an atrocious spiral of hate. There were repercussions elsewhere such as the anti-Semitic attacks in Paris in the Rue Marbeuf and the Rue des Rosiers.

It seems obvious that the last conjunction of the century, December 1994 in Scorpio, would be at the time of the Rwandan genocide in which hundreds of thousands of Tutsis, as well as some Hutus, were murdered and 700,000 refugees were faced with a war of extermination. In an about turn, there was the welcome endorsement of a former exile with the election, on May 9 1994, of the first black president of South Africa, the great Nelson Mandela. Likewise, Arafat arrived in Gaza in August 1994 as leader of the Palestinian Authority. On the negative side there was a full resumption of acts of terror: in Paris the attacks on the Saint-Michel metro and Place de l'Etoile in the summer and the Airbus crash. Moreover, there was the destabilization of the Balkans following the death of Tito in Yugoslavia. And the dark taste of the time were represented symbolically: Spielberg's film *Jurassic Park* came out and dinosaur madness seized the planet, prehistoric monsters and giant lizards took over the toy and sweet shops; goodbye to Mickey, Barbie and other sweet things that belonged to the little ones of yesteryear.

It wasn't surprising then that the attack on the US on 11 September 2001 happened when Pluto received an opposition from Saturn and quincunx from Jupiter, as Mars in Capricorn Saturn's sign applied to the Nodal axis.[9]

Chapter 6 – The Saturn–Uranus Cycle

The interval between the Saturn-Uranus conjunctions is forty-five and a half years. We will observe them spaced out through time from the mid 17th century onwards, study the last nine occurrences, always with their natural constitution in mind: dry, hard, taut, neither hot nor cold, enlisting ambition, a thirst for conquest, extremist aspirations, ventures that go to the limits, authoritarian power, the longest and most lasting reign.

1625 (mid-Leo): The rise of Cardinal Richelieu in France who, with Louis XIII, put in place the all-powerful absolute monarchy in France (1624). It came to fruition at the opposition of 1648 (when Uranus was also conjunct Neptune), with the treaties of Westphalia and Munster (1648). The supremacy of the Habsburgs came to an end; Holland and Sweden became great powers and France became the first nation of Europe. English emigration to America took place under this conjunction.

1670 (beginning of Pisces): This conjunction came at the time of the Aix-la-Chapelle Treaty (2 May 1668) with Saturn moving from Neptune to about halfway between 15° from Neptune that it has left and Uranus that it is approaching. The treaty put an end to the first War of Devolution between Spain and France. The assertion of French royal power in Europe, which Richelieu began and Mazarin completed, reached its peak. Placed at the centre of the world, Louis XIV, in his omnipotence, settled in Versailles in 1672 nevertheless he was to come up against the Triple Alliance with England, Sweden and Holland united against him. At the opposition of 1690, the European coalition drawn up against him in the War of the league of Augsburg left the Sun-King exhausted. Around this same conjunction various forms of imperialism appeared: the creation of the French East India Company 1665 and the English settlement from 1667 to 1674 of an American town which was to become New York.

1714 (mid-Virgo): The cycle was completed with the death of Louis XIV at Versailles in 1715; the end of his long reign, which brought about the Treaties of Utrecht (April 11 1714) and Rastatt (March 6 1714), and the end of the War of the Spanish Succession. France ceded the outskirts of Canada to England and Spain ceded Gibraltar. So began Great Britain's maritime and colonial supremacy. The same year, 1714, the Hanoverian dynasty of the Georges came to the English throne with George I. Meanwhile, a decadent Regency established itself in France and Prussia appeared on the European scene. At the following opposition in 1740 the great Franco-English confrontation of the Austrian War of Succession began, as well as the invasion of Silesia by Frederick II.

1761 (beginning of Aries): The end of a long era in European history: on 10 February 1763 (a Uranus-Saturn- Jupiter alignment (from 10° Aries to 4° Taurus) put an end to the Seven Years War with the Treaty of Paris. It was the ruin of the French colonial empire in North America and India, with the exception of five remaining trading posts. Great Britain became the leading maritime and colonial power cementing British imperialism. Nonetheless, at the opposition of 1782 its expansionist power reached its limit when in October 1781 its American army capitulated and the independence of the United States was established.

1805 (Mid-Libra): The First Empire in France (18 May 1804). Saturn at 24° Virgo, Uranus at 13° Libra and Jupiter at 27° Libra. Napoleon attempted to organize Europe under his imperial dynasty, establishing the Confederation of the Rhine (1806) and putting members of his family on the thrones of Europe.

1852 (beginning of Taurus): The Second Empire of Napoleon III. Prince Bonaparte, who first became president of the Second French Republic, carried out a violent coup d'état on 2 December 1851 and proclaimed himself Emperor Napoleon III on 2 December 1852. The years from 1850 to 1852 were marked by the repression of the revolutionary movements of 1848 by the sovereign autocrats in Hungary, Italy, Germany, and Austria… It was also the time of a boom in construction which led to industrial growth and the development of the capitalist economy.

1897 (End of Scorpio): The rise of imperialism. At the end of the century the imperialist nations started to assert themselves: it was not just a matter of conquering colonies but also of establishing empires. Since 1895, Russia had been engaged in the Far East and was seeking to dominate Manchuria, and Japanese imperialism also emerged at this time. British expansionism was in progress under Joseph Chamberlain and Cecil Rhodes, in southern Africa (the railway ran from the Cape to Cairo). France annexed Madagascar (1896). Déclassé, the French foreign minister, (1898) wanted to 'remake Europe', while the newspaper *French Action* was set up to feed (until the next conjunction) an aggressive extreme right ideology.

Pan-Germanism began to grow with the inauguration of the Kiel Canal (1895) and Bulow, the new chancellor (1897) launched the project that would build a railway from Bagdhad to the Persian Gulf in order to exploit Asia Minor. Pan-Americanism became fully established under President William McKinley (1897) with the Spanish-American war (1898), the annexation of Hawaii, Wake Island and the Philippines and the intervention in Panama. However, the rivalry between these imperialisms gave rise to various conflicts: Fachoda (1898) and the war between Greece and Turkey (1897).

1942 (The end of Taurus): The Second World War. Pan-Germanism successful: Hitler imposed the dictatorship of the Third Reich on the entire European continent. While, in reaction, new life was breathed into pan-Americanism with democratic intentions: America entered the Second World War in December 1941 in order to face up to Japanese aggression. The Allied victory led to the US taking the lead in world affairs.

<u>1988 (end of Sagittarius):</u> Promotion for the number 1 state. The fall of the Berlin wall in 1989 brought about the collapse of the Soviet Union and established a unipolar world. The US became the only world superpower. Its authority was omnipresent and it had a decisive weight in international life until this unilateralism is contested. There is no doubt that American imperialism has reached the summit of its historic superiority with this present cycle 1988-2032. Neo-capitalism, hand in hand with the technical revolution, brought about by computer science and crowned by the advent of the Internet.

In summary, the previous nine conjunctions in the series happened at times when the competing interests of the great powers were at their height. Having supplanted the domination of the Habsburgs, French supremacy in its turn was ousted by British ambitions, and then revived by Napoleon. Subsequently there was the harsh implementation of global imperialism, the explosion of pan-Germanism and finally the triumphant pan-Americanism. Moreover, Europe has never known such blatant authoritarians as Richelieu, Louis IV, the Holy Alliance, the two Napoleons, European autocrats and Hitler.

The Saturn-Uranus Cycles

The cycle 1805-52: United States and territorialism.
From 1803 to 1853 the United States more than tripled its size, from the purchase of Louisiana from France to the annexation of New Mexico and the Rio Grande (the Treaty of Gadsden).

The cycle 1852-97: From capitalism to imperialism
After the revolutionary turmoil of 1848 and the failure of liberal and democratic movements, Europe returned to the climate of the Holy Alliance with a return to the 1815 treaties. Reactionaries were in power everywhere. But more importantly, there was the industrial and economic

The Saturn-Uranus Cycle

revolution, which peaked in the middle of the century, when capitalism really took off.

The modernization of society mainly happened between the conjunction and the sextile, during the decade 1850 to 1860. The railway lines throughout the world went from 38,000 to 108,000 kilometres; national networks and main lines crossing Europe from one side to the other, international traffic providing regular freight services and the propeller ruling the oceans. Everything became interlinked. The discovery of the gold mines in California, Australia and New Zealand, from 1848 to 1853, revived businesses and London and Paris set themselves up as the bankers for Europe's nascent industries. The conjunction in Taurus saw the arrival of credit and of the banking establishments and a building revolution brought about rising property prices in towns. There were magnificent buildings and great blocks of houses in dressed stone, also grand shops. Bon Marché, the Louvre. England was at the forefront of this modernization as well as France at the time of the Second Empire when Paris was modernized. There was also industrialization of the Rhine-Westphalian Basin and the Saarland in Germany. The huge emigration flows from these countries to the United States in the middle of this century led to the Europeanization of the world.

Under the square of 1861-62, development in the United States was severely hampered by the animosity between the Northern and Southern states. This led to the long Civil War which didn't end until the trine. Plus there was the unfortunate Mexican war (1863) which was a fiasco on the part of Napoleon III.

The opposition lasted from 1873 to 1875. There was huge growth in the United States where they constructed as many railway lines in a few years as England had built in the last forty. But now the world was seized by a drive to speculate. From 1871 to 1873 industry and the banks lost control, resulting in a massive rise in prices and inflation. There had not been a collapse like this since the famous bankrupt John Law's Mexican bubble in 1720: the fall of all markets, bankruptcies, unemployment. In short, the economic crisis of 1873 was the greatest that century. In 1875 Europe was also troubled by a new Franco-German war and by a confrontation between England and Russia.

Around the time of the trine (1881-83) the economic situation got back on an even keel and expansionism returned: Disraeli meddled in Egypt; Jules Ferry, Prime Minister of France, in Tunisia, Tonkin and Madagascar; Bismarck, also, set foot in Africa.

Under the square (1885-1887) imperialist tensions were expressed in the various rivalries across the world. The climate was calmer at the sextile (1888-1889) when there was peace and the brilliant World Exhibition in Paris.

By the time of the conjunction in 1897, imperialism had become synonymous with national greatness: prestige and territorial expansion were the only consideration with colonial acquisitions being subsumed into empires. A brutal expansionism had been unleashed.

Cycle 1897-1942: From imperialism to fascism
Conjunction: When the Tories came to power in 1895 under Joseph Chamberlain they adopted an aggressive expansionist foreign policy. Their interventionism – the Boers, the linking of the Cape to Cairo... - exposed them to retaliation from all quarters. The most notable example was the rivalry with Russia, whose invasion of Manchuria had given rise to Japanese imperialism. Italy attempted to play a colonial role in Abyssinia but was defeated at Adwa. In France, Déclassé, at the Foreign Office on the Quai d'Orsay, praised adventurism; also in 1895, the Germans opened the Kiel Canal, the maritime route enabling their frenetic expansion into Asia Minor, etc. In addition, pan-Americanism took off in the United States (the Spanish-American War of 1898 and associated conquests) under Theodore Roosevelt with his strongly interventionist foreign policy. London and Paris were no longer at the centre of the world economy.

The Saturn-Uranus Cycle

Semi-square (1903): The Russo-Japanese War. There was a temporary economic crisis in 1903. In February 1904 the first imperialist confrontation took place with the Russo-Japanese War and Anglo-German rivalry worsened.

Sextile (1905-06): Entente Cordiale and US growth. In Western Europe there was a resumption of economic activity and the Anglo-German rivalry brought England and France together. They ratified an entente cordiale in 1904 that charted the future of Europe. In the United States, Theodore Roosevelt enlarged the great republic's sphere of influence by confirming the doctrine of pan-Americanism.

Square (1909-10): The first signs of war in Europe. Europe seized by war fever. In 1908-09 the Bosnian crisis erupted, followed in 1910 by unrest in Macedonia which lit a touchpaper in the Balkans. Also, there was the Agadir affair the following year which put all embassies on high alert. The Balkan wars were to be a prelude to the First World War.

Trine (1912-13): The liberal world was judged to be at its height. Nothing else, apparently, other than that society was beefing up on all sides with an enormous industrial machine being built for the production of armaments. The world was on the brink. The summer of 1914, when conflict broke out, fell on the sesquiquadrate in the cycle, the war lasting for the duration of the Uranus-Neptune opposition, almost spanned by the hemicycle which Jupiter made travelling from one planet to the other.

Opposition (1918-20): The transfer of world economic power from Europe to America. The entry of the United States into the war fell under the quincunx but it was at the start of the opposition that General Pershing's American troops received a baptism of fire in their first offensive at Argonne in the summer of 1918. This tragedy of war was to cause the world of capital to move its centre of gravity. Having always borrowed from Europe, the United States became the great giver of credit and from now on played the role of the world's banker, especially for the impoverished European countries who were economically exhausted.

Trine (1925-27): Recovery and prosperity. In 1924, the economy was stabilized by the Dawes Plan and various reforms in central Europe and, furthermore, Great Britain returned to the gold standard. From 1925, economic activity accelerated. The old continent was full of vitality and enjoyed prosperity, the ordeal of the Great War almost forgotten. Financial and economic expansionism was widespread with America experiencing fabulous growth.

Square (1930-31): Economic crisis. Everything was called into question by the economic crisis of 1929-32 which affected the whole world (except the USSR). Most notably, Great Britain abandoned the gold standard. The United States was affected the most with 11 million unemployed in October 1932 (a tenth of the population) and industrial production below the standard of living for 1929.

Sextile (1934-35): Recovery. Various national experiments (the New Deal in the United States), a general recovery from 1933 was sustained for two more years.

Semi-square (1937): A dip. A general climate of stagnation: slow down, deflation, devaluation.

Conjunction (May 1942 at 29° Taurus): The Second World War and fascism. The world plunged into a new international conflagration. Pan-Germanism, which had a brilliant start at the conjunction and which foundered at the opposition, now triumphed: Germany imposed a Nazi dictatorship on Europe until its fall.

Cycle 1942-88: The Americanization of the world
Conjunction: The United States, military and political superpower. At the same time as Germany was exercising its power that of the United States was taking shape. Pan-Americanism had ended at the previous conjunction in 1897. At the opposition of 1919 it became the world's largest economy while regressively refusing to join the League of Nations. But having been isolationist at the opposition of 1920 it was now necessary to totally engage with the international scene. At this conjunction the United States plunged into the Second World War at the centre of the

melee. The weight of their, soon, superior military force added to their political authority which was evident when the Atlantic Charter was established (26 August 1941) followed by the United Nations Declaration (1 January 1942) which established a new world organization. The conditions had been set in place for the world to be Americanized by the end of the cycle.

Semi-square (September 1946-July 1947): The beginning of the Cold War. The World War over, the USSR, a former ally, became the new enemy. During 1946 tension mounted between the two adversaries until it reached breaking point with the adoption of the Truman doctrine giving military aid to Greece and Turkey (12 March 1947) followed by the Marshall plan (5 June 1947) which gave economic assistance to Western Europe. The world divided into two hostile blocs and a Cold War began between the opposing countries. Also, the Latin American states became politically unsatisfactory and the McCarthy witch-hunt began.

Sextile (September 1948-June 1949): The Atlantic Alliance (NATO). A defence system organized between the United States and Western Europe. On 4 April 1949 the Atlantic Pact was signed, which brought twelve countries together in NATO. Previously the idea of pan-Americanism had been affirmed at the international conference in Bogotá, where on 30 April 1948 twenty-oneAmerican republics had signed the Charter of the Organization of American States. Thus to defend against communist subversion the western bloc placed itself under the hegemony of the US.

Square (December 1951-October 1952): The Korean War. The war in Korea took place under this aspect, communist North Korea attacked South Korea on 25 June 1950, resulting in an immediate American intervention under the mandate of the UN. A hot episode in the Cold War and when China also intervened there were fears that the conflict would spread. The armistice of Pan Mun Jon of 27 July 1953 put an end to a match that ended in a draw. In addition the US insistence on the rearming of Germany disturbed the European Community and there were also various disturbances in Iran and Egypt.

Trine (January 1956-October 1957): The Eisenhower Doctrine. The aspect was already close to 3° in February 1955 when the Bagdad Pact was signed (24 February 1955), an American defence system which reinforced the Atlantic Pact that had been put in place at the sextile. A climate of détente was on the horizon with a conference of the four great powers in Geneva the following July; the first signs of a thaw. In addition in July 1956 the presidents of 18 American republics (out of 21) confirmed that there was solidarity between them in their approach to world affairs. In January 1957, the Eisenhower Doctrine established American power in the Middle East, confirmed by the Suez crisis (the Franco-English intervention which came to a halt in November 1956) where the interests of the two great powers converged.

Opposition (April 1965-January 1967): The Vietnam War and race riots. In February 1965 the US intervened in the Vietnam War with military bombardments, and then in June by engaging marines on the ground until there were half a million men by 1968. There were 57,000 dead and 30,000 wounded, the country's morale was shaken and there was no victory. Especially as the war was accompanied by urban race riots that produced an atmosphere of civil war: there were 43 in 1966 and 164 in 1967 (the time of Stokely Carmichael and Malcolm X). There were also challenges from around the world with Latin America taken over by the revolutionaries of Che Guevara's Tricontinental.

Sesquiquadrate (July 1970-May 1971): Locked into the Vietnam War by expanding the military intervention into Cambodia in April 1970 and Laos in the following August, then in February 1971: without result. There was tension between America and Europe and a monetary crisis which erupted in August 1971.

Trine (July 1972-May 1973): General détente. Having come with the opposition, the Vietnam War ends at the trine. The quadripartite agreement on Berlin was signed in September 1971 (6° orb). Then came President Nixon's visit to Peking in February 1972, making peace with China which had been implicated in the conflict in Vietnam. Then his visit to Moscow in May where he signed a charter of détente (SALT 1 Accord): the gesture was followed by a visit to the United States by Brezhnev in June 1973. Meanwhile the accords that put an end to the American war in Vietnam were signed in Paris on 23 January 1973.

Square (October 1975-July 1976): Flawed government. After Watergate, the weakness continued under Gerald Ford and then Jimmy Carter, American politics started to slip, flanked by a timid Congress. This climate was accompanied by a slow down in growth, inflation and a trade deficit. When the Portugese colonies were liberated on the death of Salazar the USSR took the opportunity to invest massively in Africa and it kept its grip on Eastern Europe.

Sextile (September 1979-July 1980): Regaining control. Following the ratification of the diplomatic links with communist China on 15 December 1978 (5° orb), a second accord was signed in Vienna on 18 June 1979 by the superpowers on the limitation of strategic weapons (SALT 2), in keeping with the previous one at the time of the trine. Also, because of the Soviet intervention in Afghanistan in December 1979, there were various reactions including a campaign to put Ronald Reagan in the White House to provide effective policies.

Semi-square (October 1981-July 1982): Economic crisis and euro-missiles. Growth and productivity were at an all-time low. In a climate of recession an armaments conference in Geneva which opened on 30 November 1981, ended in failure opening the way to the dangerous installation of Euro-missiles.

Cycle 1988-2032 : Globalization

Conjunction (February-October 1988): The trio of three Saturn-Uranus, Saturn-Neptune and Uranus-Neptune, signalled a pivotal time with huge changes in world history, even civilization. This was indeed the case when first the Berlin Wall came down and this was followed by the collapse of the Soviet empire. It was the end of the bipolar world which had dominated the previous half-century: only one of the two would be victorious. This was the beginning of a new situation in which the single global leadership of the United States would prevail: the world would now develop under the Stars and Stripes. If communism disappeared from history, neo-capitalism would be supreme. At the same time there was an enormous wave of American economic growth and commercial multilateral negotiations were established in connection with the electronic revolution, crowned by the Internet, which contributed to the progress of world development.

Semi-square (May1994-February 1995): In December 1994 Mexico was on the verge of national bankruptcy. The peso crisis shook the international monetary system.

Sextile (May 1996-May 1997): In place of GATT, the WTO (World Trade Organization) held its first ministerial conference in Singapore in December 1996, and obtained immediate results. Notably there was the agreement to abolish customs duty on technology products (300 innovative products). The agreement involved 39 countries and was strengthened by another agreement on 15 February 1997 about the liberalization of telecommunication services (telephone, telex, fax, cables); the 69 counties who signed represented 93% of worldwide turnover; an explosion of globalization.

Square (July 1999-May 2000): A North-South divide emerged with a challenge to the hegemony of the powerful nations in a debate about how the ongoing globalization was to be governed. This was followed by the fiasco of the WTO summit in Seattle (30 November-3 December 1999) and while this was in progress the first social world forum took place at Porto Alegre in Brazil from 25 to 30th January 2001 (square with a 4° orb), the start of the anti-globalization movement. Remember also that economic growth stalled at that time, shaken by the bursting of the Internet bubble in March 2000.

Trine (August 2002-June 2003): The ministerial confer-ence of the WTO in Doha from the 9 to 13 November 2001 (6° orb) enshrined the importance of China's membership of that body and a new cycle of negotiations was launched called the Development Round. This time the interests of the developing countries were to be given preference. There followed a series of international meetings, which ran from March to August, under the egis of the WTO, about giving aid for development. This stimulus happened at the same time as a revival in American economic growth from 2003-04. It was under this trine that America invaded Iraq.

Sesquiquadrate (August 2004-June 2005): The ongoing intervention in Iraq turned sour with the giant losing its hold in the fight against terrorism, and furthermore there was a new upsurge in anti-globalization protests.

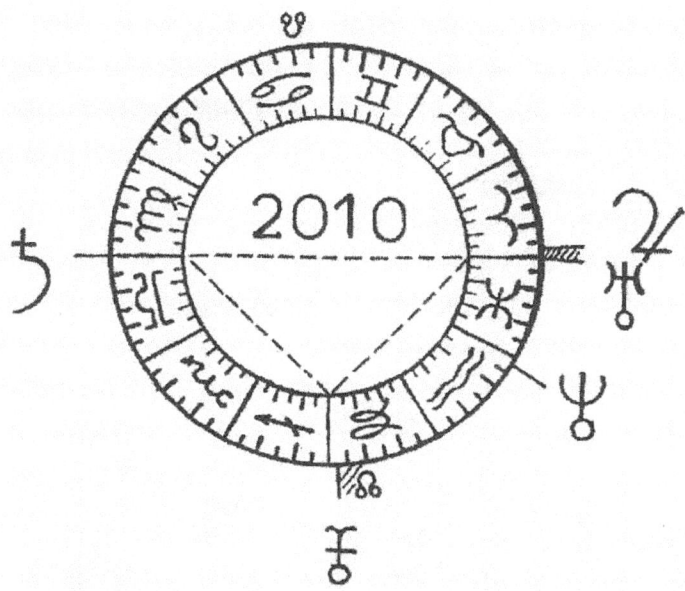

Opposition (November 2008-September 2009): A highly charged configuration with Jupiter joining Uranus in opposition to Saturn from May 2010 to March 2011. It was natural to expect the critical turn of events, which having already begun with economic and financial disturbances in the US in 2008, erupted in Europe when the Sun transited Saturn in September 2009. There was an economic super-crisis and, what's more, a disastrous systemic crisis, with a financial storm that destabilized Europe: countries like Greece, on the edge of bankruptcy, were made to put in place rigorous measures and with the euro devalued, the continent became the 'soft underbelly' of the world.

As if that was not bad enough there was a run of extraordinary natural disturbances and exceptionally bad weather. The Icelandic volcano caused 95,000 flights to be cancelled and left 7 million passengers stranded for a week. Under the Jupiter-Uranus conjunction in Aries, influenced by a square to Pluto, a revolution broke out in the Arab world and overtook a number of African countries (Tunisia, Egypt, Libya, Syria. I wrote about the arrival of such a general upheaval in number 92 of *L'astrologue* 4th trimester 1990: 'a special 21st century number'.

Chapter 7 - The Saturn-Neptune Cycle

The speed of their sidereal revolutions, 29 years for the first and 164 years for the latter, means that Saturn-Neptune conjunctions occur every 35-36 years and move forward two or three signs each time. Before I give a résumé of the last six conjunctions I will first outline the basic features.

With the Jupiter-Saturn couple, the first represents the wealth and the second the work done, profit and labour. There is a real contrast between the energetic and dramatic duo Jupiter-Uranus, with its affinity to the MC, and the deep nocturnal couple Saturn-Neptune, which is in keeping with the opposite IC; power and prosperity above and misfortune and poverty below. But when hunger brings the wolf out of the forest, human need increases the collective demands of a frustrated population which has no hope. So this conjunction is about popular insurrections that are usually fired by ideological beliefs.

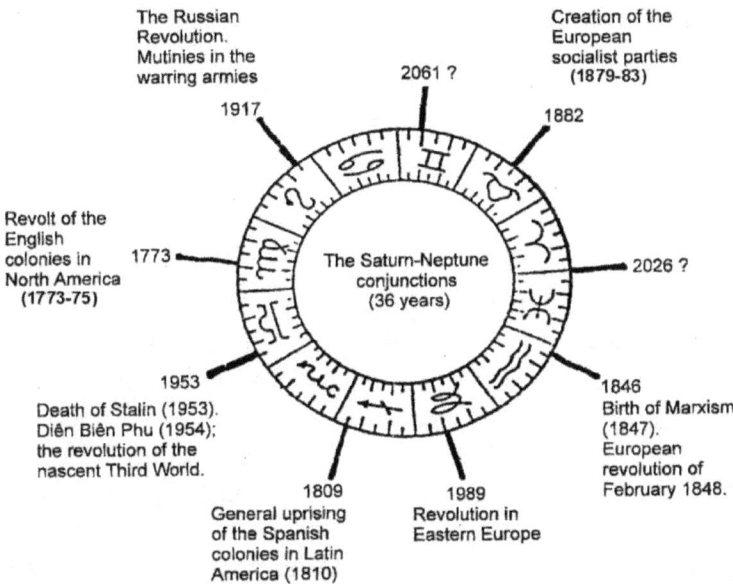

Other configurations reflecting the revolutionary current: the Saturn-Neptune opposition under which, notably, the French Revolution evolved.

Conjunction 1773 (21° Virgo): The Boston Tea Party of 16-17 December 1773 [see chart below]: a conjunction with a 5° orb which is also opposed by Jupiter; this trio was aligned on the axis of the Moon's nodes and on these days was also squared by a Sun-Mercury-Mars conjunction. This was the starting point of the revolt that took place in the thirteen English colonies in North America, which ended with the United States becoming independent in 1776.

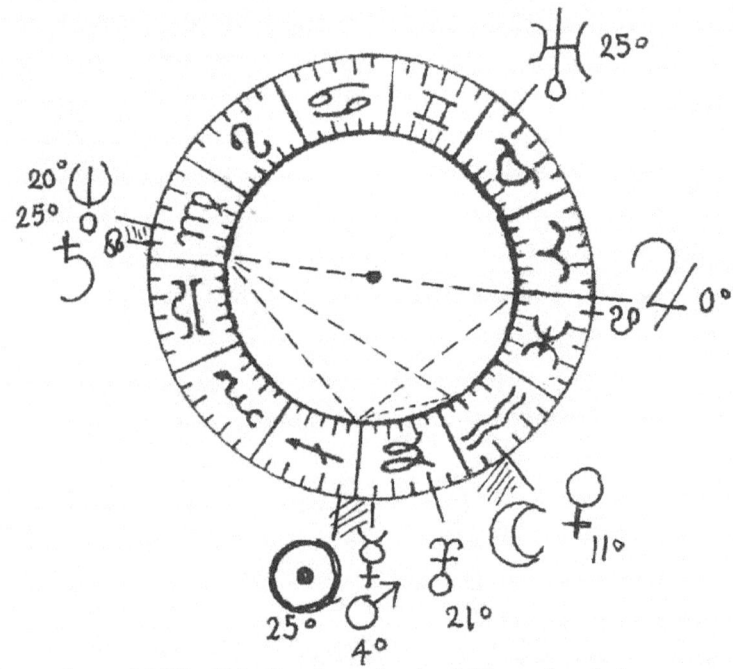

Conjunction 1809 (6° Sagittarius): What had happened in North America also took place in South America. In 1810 there was a general uprising in the Spanish colonies of Latin America: Venezuela, Argentina, Chile, and Mexico, which, eventually, at the end of a long struggle led to their independence. As well as this there was the upheaval of the Napoleonic campaigns (the Peninsular War and others) which led to a resurgence of European nationalism. This was the cause of the Spanish and Portuguese colonies becoming emancipated. The occupation of the Iberian Peninsula (Joseph, brother of Napoleon, was on the Spanish throne)

The Saturn-Neptune Cycle

meant that the colonies had to administrate themselves and from 1810 Hidalgo and Morales signalled their independence.

<u>Conjunction 1846 (26° Aquarius)</u>: The arrival of Marxism. In 1847 the 'Communist League' was created with its first congress and the Communist Party Manifesto by Marx and Engels was launched. As well as this, 14 months after the conjunction (14° orb), but under the Sun's punctual arrival at 26° Aquarius, and helped by a square aspect from Mars, for two weeks in February unprecedented revolutionary movements took hold of the European continent. They were simultaneously patriotic, unitarian, liberal or proletarian according to the country concerned. In two weeks this movement had inflamed nearly every country: France, Germany, Italy, Austria, Hungary, Bavaria, United Kingdom, the Danish dukedoms: there were uprisings, petitions, marches, public and worker unrest. In France, a Parisian insurrection overthrew the king, Louis-Philippe (22-25 February), and proclaimed a proletarian-style Second Republic with a humanitarian philosophy.

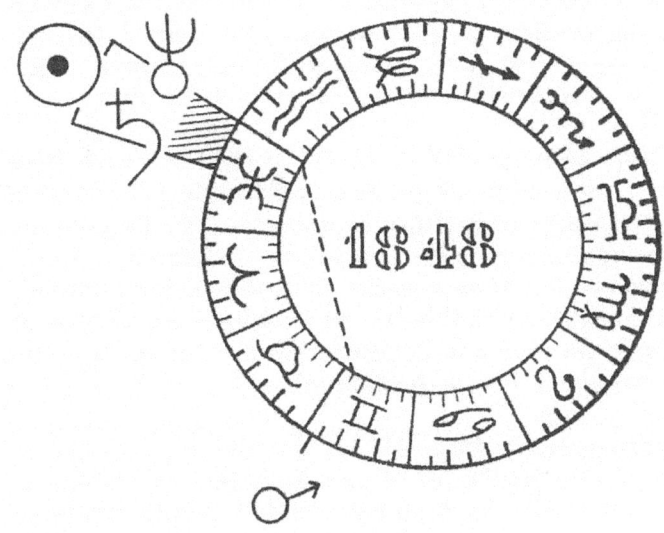

Conjunction 1882 (16° Taurus): The birth of the European socialist parties. After numerous small starts, a Marxist group called The Emancipation of Labour was founded in Geneva in 1883 by Plekhanov, Lavrov (Zassoulitch) and Axelrod. A Marxist party, the French Workers Party, was founded in France in 1880 with Jules Guesde and Paul Lafargue. In England, Henry Mayers Hyndman founded a socialist party, the Social Democratic Federation, and at the same time the Fabian Society was created whose early members were Sidney and Beatrice Webb and George Bernard Shaw. In future years this led to the development of the Labour Party. In France, an important law, the first of its kind, on social security, was passed in 1883. Belgium already had a socialist party which was created in 1879, as had Germany. René Raymond in *The XIXth Century* (Le Seuil, 1974) summarized the situation: 'In the 1880's, in Italy, Spain, Belgium, Holland and Scandinavia socialist parties arose which were allied to Marxism.', Since then these parties have sought power by putting forward candidates for election in various countries.

Conjunction of 1917 (4° Leo): The Russian Revolution. The Bolshevik Party seized power in Russia on 7 November 1917 and the country fell into the hands of the Soviets. Similarly, in May the armies fighting in the First World War mutinied. Also Latin America underwent a revolutionary awakening around the time of the conjunction, from the Chilean Socialist Congress in September 1915 to the Pan-American Socialist Conference in Buenos Aires in April 1919.

Conjunction of 1952-53 (21°-22° Libra): The death in March 1953 of Stalin, so long in power in Russia, opened a new chapter in Soviet history as if the clock had been turned back to zero. Communism gained ground and came out of isolation in supporting the cause of de-colonialization which, with the Afro-Asiatic nationalists was in progress in the Third World. Also the first Latin American workers revolution took place in Bolivia in 1952-53.

Conjunction of 1989 (10° Capricorn): with an opposition from Jupiter: the fall of the Berlin wall on the 9 November 1989, with the immediate collapse of the 'popular democracies' in Eastern Europe which underwent a total revolution; then followed by the demise of the Soviet Union itself in December 1991; the collapse of an historic empire.

Cycle 1846-1882: birth of Marxism to revolutionary parties
At the conjunction of December 1846 as the doctrine of communism was taken up worldwide, Europe was consumed by the revolutionary fever of February 1848. The movement was suppressed, but the embers continued to smoulder. Even so the workers' movement did not reappear until the trine (the pressure of strikes) because of the economic crisis of 1857.

Opposition (November 1862-September 1863): Ideological discord. The working class went through a difficult phase from 1862 to 1864. In 1863, Lassalle created the 'General German Workers Association'. The same year workers associations emerged in Paris and for the first time the signatories to a manifesto proposed that the trade union leaders organize a general association which, on September 28 1864, became the First International. But there was discord due to the difficult circumstances.

Trine (1869): It wasn't until the trine that the International as a power began to appeal to the rapidly growing workers movements in 1869-1870 and it was the same with the first elections of republicans. Women's unions also emerged at this time.

Square (January 1873): torn by internal divisions, the fragile Internationale, which began at the opposition, imploded at the congress of September 1872, when both Bakounine and James Guillaume were excluded and it became a mere shadow of its former self.

Sextile (all 1876): General awakening. It was Russia that took the first steps in founding the 'Southern Union of Russian Workers'. In Germany a number of groups merged into the Socialist Workers' Party, with Liebnecht and Bebel, while in France a Parisian congress put some life into the movement, even though the working class was not represented politically.

Conjunction (May 1882): The effect of this awakening was the founding of the great socialist parties of the world. The Belgian Socialist Party had already been set up in Brussels in 1879 and was soon followed by a Spanish party. In France, a workers' congress in Marseilles in October 1879 brought Jules Guesde to prominence. It was under his auspices that a national socialist party was constituted. In Great Britain, in 1881, Hydman founded Democracy, a Marxist-inspired federation, while in 1883 the Fabian Society gathered together intellectuals who were interested in socialism. On 15 November 1881 the American Federation of Labour was created in Pittsburgh. And Plekhanov founded the first Russian Marxist group: the Emancipation of Labour.

Cycle 1882-1917: European socialist parties & the Russian revolution

Conjunction: At the beginning of this cycle the large western countries had their respective socialist parties or unions. The pressure they brought to bear on those in power brought about the first social legislation and the organization of labour. There was legal protection for women and children and, what was most necessary, the monitoring of hazardous industries... Even in those early years Germany introduced social security and other counties followed with something similar.

Sextile (1887-88): The socialist and unionist movements began to take shape. In 1889 this led to the foundation of the Second Internationale with its inspirational ideas of a better life.

Trine (1892-93): The movement gained in strength during these years. In France, following the elections in 1893, forty members were at last elected to the Chamber of Deputies where Jaures acted as their leader and the same year the General Confederation of Labour was created and got off to a good start. Since 1890 thirty-five socialists had sat in the Reichstag in Germany; likewise in 1892 the first Labour candidate was elected to the House of Commons in London and helped found the Labour Party the following year. Also in 1893, Lenin began his political career in St Petersburg.

Opposition (February-October 1889) The year that socialist ideology suffered major splits. In France alliances were broken because for the first time a socialist (Millerand) became a minister in Waldeck-Rousseau's government and this resulted in a split between Jaures and Guesde. Then a Marxist revisionist movement made an appearance and Bernstein's *Evolutionist Socialism* was published. And in Russia the cracks that appeared in the relationship between Lenin, who wanted to consolidate the revolutionary movement, and the Plekhanov-Martov group, ended in a Bolshevik Menshevik split.

Trine (1906-07): As well as the trine from Saturn Neptune received an exact opposition from Uranus and was transited by Jupiter. During this harmonious passage the struggles of working people brought about social advances. In France in 1906 the syndicalist movement, at its conference in Amiens, agreed on the basis for its actions, while radicals and socialists were winning elections. In Great Britain, 1906 was the year that the Labour Party appeared and won twenty-nine parliamentary seats; the General Confederation of Labour was set up in Italy and socialists won a good number of seats in Austria-Hungary in the 1907 elections.

Square (1909-10): Syndicalism in crisis (the resignation of Griffuelhes in France). Almost everywhere workers were engaged in difficult struggles: the postal workers in France, the dockers in England.

Sextile (1912): The German Party became the most powerful in the Reichstag, and the Bolsheviks were victorious in the elections to the fourth Duma.

Conjunction (August 1917): Europe was exhausted by the Great War which was still ongoing. In the spring there were mutinies in the armies of both camps with fraternization in the trenches; there was an atmosphere of revolt among the soldiers. The bubble burst in Russia when in November the revolution put the Bolsheviks in power.

Cycle 1917-53: From the Russian Revolution to the end of the Stalinist era

Conjunction (August 1917): The October revolution. The Soviets took power on 17 November 1917 and installed a dictatorship of the proletariat under the direction of the Bolshevik Party with Lenin and Trotsky. The country became prey to civil war, made worse by the intervention of foreign armies which isolated it from the world. The times were critical for 'military communism'.

Semi-square (October 1921): Chaos and the NEP It was the most critical chaotic year. Besides typhus, which was spreading, millions of people were hit by famine, and agricultural and industrial production fell to their lowest levels. In March the insurrection at Kronstadt shook a government that was still to evolve. Soon after, a series of decrees set up the New Economic Policy NEP which was a return to economic liberalism in order to learn the practicalities of power.

Sextile (December 1922-September 1923): Having overcome chaos and war, the regime stabilized. With the country's borders settled, the Union of Soviet Socialist Republics (USSR) signed a treaty on 30 December 1922 forming a federal state with its powers defined by the constitution of July 1923. In the meantime the regime was recognized by numerous countries including the United States, United Kingdom, Italy, France and Japan while the conferences of Genoa and The Hague (1922) marked the entry of the Soviets into international life.

Square (January-November 1926): The Stalinist dictatorship. The death of Lenin in 1924 opened the way for a power struggle and in particular the conflict between Trotsky and Stalin. From 1925 to 1927 a close fight between these two rivals resulted in Trotsky's expulsion and exile, and Stalin forcing the notables of the regime to submit to his dictatorship.

Trine (March- December 1929): The Five-Year Plan. In 1928 Russia was still a backward country with wooden ploughs, like countries in the West at the beginning of the 20th century. Stalin introduced the first five-year plan which was executed in October 1928. Enormous tasks were undertaken: frenzied industrialization and huge agricultural collectives. This titanic development of the means of production allowed him to catch up and close a gap that had been there for centuries. At a time when capitalism was collapsing in an unprecedented economic crisis, this 'socialist construction' allowed the USSR to become a new power in world markets and to present itself as a strong state.

Semi-square (February-December 1931): Difficulties on the farms. The collectivisation of the countryside entered a critical phase. This was a year of bad harvests which caused a farmers' revolt and a delay in land reform.

Opposition (March 1936-January 1937): The Moscow trials, Anti-Comintern Pact, Spanish revolution, Popular Front. In the ascendant phase of the cycle the second Five-Year Plan (1933-37) allowed the USSR to attain the third or fourth rung among the industrial powers of the world, but now the regime, as it acknowledged, was in acute crisis. A secret struggle was raging in the heart of the party in which the old Bolsheviks of 1917 were forced to form a clandestine opposition to the Stalinist clan. The 'old guard' communists were decimated with the Moscow trials where sixteen of the accused, all big names, appeared before the supreme military court on 19 August 1936 (Zinoviev, Kamenev, Smirnov...). And on 23 January 1937 a second Moscow trial began with Rykov and Bukharin, which liquidated the military high command including Tukhachevski and seven marshals and generals. Across the world the working class was experiencing a significant revival. Between 1934 and 1938 a mass movement took off in the United States and in May 1936 the Popular Front came on the scene in France. But equally barriers were put up against communism with Franco's counter-revolution in Spain in July 1936 and the signing of the Anti-Comintern Pact on 25 November 1936 by Germany, Japan and Italy.

Sesqui-quadrate (May 1940-March 1941): The war. Despite its efforts to escape the threat of the Anti-Comintern Pact, 22 June 1941, the USSR was attacked by Nazi Germany and its European partners.

Trine (July 1941-April 1942): Military resistance with an Anglo-American-Soviet alliance. The blitzkrieg launched by Hitler's Reich against the USSR failed when the Wehrmacht was brought to a halt outside Moscow in November 1941. Soviet power, with British and American aid, prevailed in battle; so much so that the victory of the Red Army over the Wehrmacht augmented the prestige of the USSR which emerged from the ordeal a greater nation.

Square (July 1944-April 1945): The end of allied solidarity and a climate of revolutionary crisis. The war over, the Allies broke up. Since the beginning of 1945 conflicts had begun to emerge with the advance of the Red Army into Eastern Europe where it installed pro-communist authorities. On 18 January 1945 a provisional government in Poland was imposed on the Allies. Pressure with menace was put on Turkey. Besides the liberation of the countries in the east, from the autumn, there were revolutionary movements in Greece, Belgium, Yugoslavia and Italy; but of all these efforts only Yugoslavia became communist.

Sextile (July 1947): Economic recovery and the formation of the Cominform. The fourth Five-Year Plan was put into effect from 1946 to 1949: the enormous devastation caused by the war was erased. In addition, the countries in the Soviet zone evolved governmental regimes that were in coalition with those of the Soviet bloc. While on 22 September 1947 the Cominform, which consisted of the 'Popular Democracies', was put in place between autumn 1947 and spring 1948: Bulgaria, Romania, East Germany, Czechoslovakia, Poland, Hungary, Yugoslavia - a Soviet stranglehold on central and eastern Europe. There was also the communist victory for Mao Tse-tung in China.

Semi-square (August 1948): The Yugoslavian crisis and the Berlin Blockade. First cracks in the Soviet bloc: faced with this new united front Tito's Yugoslavia refused to become a 'satellite' country. This resistance to Stalin ended in a split between Moscow and Belgrade on 29 June 1948 and the unity of the communist world was shattered. The same month the terrible Berlin Blockade began which lasted nearly a year. It was also the time of the Lysenko affair and the death of Zhdanov.

At the end of the Sun-Venus-Jupiter conjunction a treaty of friendship was signed by the USSR and communist China on 14 February 1950: a pact that brought together these two great communist countries. Saturn was then at 17° of Virgo between Pluto at 16° Leo and Neptune at 17° Libra, with the result that he semi-sextile (30°) between Saturn and Neptune was united with the semi-sextile between Saturn and Pluto, Saturn-Pluto being the cycle of Chinese communism

Conjunction (November 1952-July 1953): The death of Stalin on the 5 March 1953 surprised the world and was not without some mourning.

Cycle 1953-89: De-Stalinization to the fall of the U.S.S.R.

Conjunction: The death of Stalin. After almost three decades in power as an absolute dictator this historic break felt like the end of an era. The reverberations from the rupture led to an interior shake-up. A collective leadership followed that wanted to loosen the grip of the dictatorship but they were unable to prevent a revolutionary outbreak in June: there were troubles in Czechoslovakia, riots in Poland, an insurrection in East Berlin. After a period of confusion Nikita Khrushchev emerged and his first measures created a thaw and started the process of de-Stalinization. However there were still troubles in Poland and Hungary. In addition, in 1954 and especially after the Conference of Bandung in April 1955, a revolutionary movement began. This time the ideology was that of the Third World, with Nasser, Nehru, Sukarno and Tito as its leaders. It was an international third force, dedicated to the ongoing decolonization, something that brings to mind the previous conjunctions of 1773 and 1809. They formed a neutral front with close connections to Moscow.

Semi-square (December 1957): Purge. In June 1957 there was a failed attempt to remove Khrushchev from the Presidium. This was followed by the expulsion from the Soviet leadership of an 'Anti-Party Group' (Molotov, Malenkov, Kaganovitch...), with Zhukov being dismissed in the autumn. This was the end of the Stalinist old guard. A de-Stalinization in which power was torn between Yugoslavian 'revisionism' (a reconciliation with Tito having taken place) and Chinese 'dogmatism', with the first differences between Moscow and Peking appearing in November 1957. This was also the time of a hardening in relations over the Nobel Prize being awarded to Pasternak.

Sextile (March-December 1959): Growth and coexistence. At the end of the decade the economic potential of the country grew rapidly in all sectors and industrial production was two and a half times that of 1950. From 1958 onwards the USSR with its technological superiority was confirmed as a new power. It became a world leader in the space race (Sputnik...). At the same time, ever since the Geneva Conference of 13 July 1959, international relations had been improving. The following September the Soviet Premier made an unprecedented official visit to the United States and the Camp David USSR and the US that opened the door to peaceful coexistence.

Square (February 1963): The Cuban Missile Crisis and schism between Moscow and Peking. At the end of October 1962 tension between the two great powers came to a head with the delivery of Soviet missiles to Cuba. Washington and Moscow were on the brink of a third world war. Furthermore since the autumn of 1962 a conflict on the Sino-Indian border created a schism between Moscow and Peking. After a Soviet letter written on 30 March, followed by a Chinese response on 14 June, the rupture was confirmed at the Moscow talks which took place between 6 and 20 July 1963. The worldwide communist movement then split with China forming a second revolutionary front.

Trine (June 1965-November 1966): Peaceful coexistence. The new team of Brezhnev and Kosygin, in power since October 1964, endorsed the policy of detente and understanding which Khrushchev had introduced. It was the USSR no less, that found a solution to the ongoing war between India and Pakistan with the parties being reconciled in January 1966 in Tashkent. A trip to the Soviet Union by De Gaulle, followed by Kosygin's visit to Paris in December 1966, contributed to the rapprochement between East and West. In January 1967 this atmosphere led to the Outer Space Treaty, signed by 107 nations, which was about the demilitarization of space. (Jupiter had joined Saturn and Neptune to form a grand trine.) At home, the 28th Congress of April 1966 dedicated itself to improving the standard of living, in a time of economic prosperity. A wind of liberalization was blowing through the European socialist camp.

Sesquiquadrate (May 1967-March 1968): A jarring note. This expansion got out of hand with the appearance of the Soviet fleet in the Mediterranean, an early intervention in the conflict in the Middle East, and the pernicious incursion of the Prague Spring. Moreover the youthful left wing revolt of '68' in France marginalized Soviet socialism.

Opposition (June 1971-April 1972): From the full height of its power to the decline of the regime. The USSR was at its height. In its expansionist times its zone of influence stretched from Cairo (the Egyptian–Soviet Friendship Treaty of 27 May 1971) via Delhi (the Indian-Soviet Friendship Treaty 9 August 1971) to Hanoi, the Soviet fleet sailed in every ocean and the Red Army had never been so powerful. Yet already with the Moon landing on 20 July 1969, the Americans had overtaken the Soviets in the space race and it didn't really matter that the flame of world revolution had been passed to the Maoists because when a spent regime goes into decline the rot comes from within. In 1970 Andréi Sakharov founded the Moscow Human Rights Committee while the same year Solzhenitsyn blew away the illusions of progressive ideals. And there was an uprising of Polish workers on the Baltic in December 1970 at the gates of the Soviet state.

Semi-square (July 1975-May 1976): A historic compromise. There was a new attack on the Soviet hegemony and on communist centralism at the pan-European conference in Berlin on 29 and 30th June 1976 by the Italian Enrico Berlinguer and Santiago Carrillo of Spain who together formed a European party.

Trine (September 1976-June 1977): Last growth. The USSR pursued peaceful expansion in the continent of Africa in 1977, notably by investing in Cuba and peacefully bringing Angola, Ethiopia and the Yemen into the Soviet camp. Small fry!

Square (September 1979-June 1980): Afghanistan, SS-20's and Solidarity. The Red Army invaded Afghanistan on 24 September 1979. It was the start of a long and fruitless war. More importantly the Soviets installed SS-20 missiles in Eastern Europe, a strategy that brought them to the brink. On 30 August 1980 after a series of strikes the Polish state recognized Walesa's Solidarity: a decision that was followed by the resignation of the First Secretary of the Polish Communist Party on 5 September. The popular uprising had succeeded and this concession to free trade unionism undermined the foundations of the communist parties in the popular democracies.

Sextile (October 1982-July 1983): This was a time of containment and of the disintegration of the Soviet bastion. On 30 November 1981 (5° orb), in an atmosphere of fear, a conference about Euro missiles opened in Geneva and this led to the beginning of the START (reduction in armaments) talks on 29 June1982. Yuri Andropov, who succeeded Leonid Brezhnev who died on 10 November 1982, strengthened diplomacy but the USSR was an inert force and would not move

Semi-square (January–September 1984): The regime began a spectacular downward slide with the deaths of

President Andropov on 8 February 1984 and then his successor Konstantin Chernenko in March 1985. Their role was assumed by their successor, Mikhail Gorbachev, who made tentative reforms, but it was much too late.

<u>Conjunction</u> (March-November 1989): This conjunction at 10-11° Capricorn was amplified, like that of 1748, by an opposition from Jupiter. A wind of revolution was blowing throughout the world and the USSR was swept away. It is worth retracing its history.

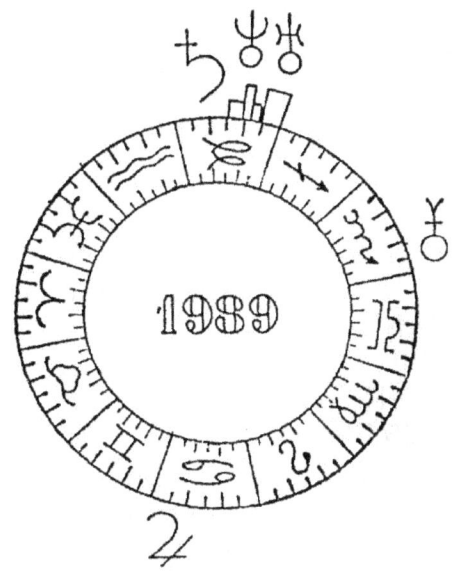

It all started with the explosion of the 'Beijing Spring'. Student demonstrations began on 17 April 1989 in Beijing. On the 25-26 demonstrations were prohibited, and this provoked a march of a million students in the Chinese capital the next day. After that the various processions converged and a million people marched every day... until the massacre on the night of 3-4. June But there were people marching in solidarity in their millions in Canton, Shanghai, Hong Kong, Moscow and in the European capitals.

A national peculiarity: The Chinese Communist Party came into being between 30 June and 1 July 1921 under a Sun- Mars- Pluto conjunction at 7°-8° Cancer. When the party seized power and established the People's Chinese Republic on 1 October 1949, Uranus at 5° Cancer was transiting the position of this initial conjunction. Now, at the Beijing Spring, it is this triple conjunction of the party (later joined by Uranus when the regime was created) that the 1989 Uranus follows the 1989 Neptune and Saturn in making an exact opposition.[10]

Poland was first to arrive at the party in April. Solidarity obtained the accords which led to the first non-communist government on 12 September. The breach had opened. Hungary followed suit when they obtained a similar result on 13 June and the dismantling of the Iron Curtain along the Austrian border. This triggered a mass exodus of East Germans over the summer, with those who didn't leave pouring on to the streets to demonstrate. The collapse of the GDR's regime was precipitated by a visit from Gorbachev on the 7 October. Abandoned by the Soviets, Erich Honecker left power on 18 October. It was after that that the Berlin Wall fell on the 9 November. The point of no return. Bulgaria, Czechoslovakia, Yugoslavia all followed. And finally Romania itself with the deaths of the Ceauescu couple on 25 December when the Sun passed over the great conjunction; with the exception of Albania, the whole communist bloc of 'popular democracies' had gone!

Again, at the end of this same year the Lithuanian communist party broke away, there were demonstrations in Mongolia which also seceded and a civil war in Azerbaijan, and all were caused by the break-up of the empire. The final death blow awaiting the regime was the failed Moscow putsch on 19 August 1991, which caused the collapse of the KGB and the Communist Party of the Soviet Union, as well as the public statues belonging to the regime. This precipitated the race to independence of the USSR's provinces, all signalling the end of communist power. (All reflected by a cocktail of conjunctions, Sun-Mercury-Venus-Jupiter sesquiquadrates to Neptune.) What followed was the creation of the Commonwealth of Independent States (CIS) on 13 December 1991. Saturn was already some

The Saturn-Neptune Cycle

distance from Neptune at 18° but all of this historic turning point came under the auspices of this conjunction.

I made my first forecast concerning this historic turning point in the destiny of the Soviet Union at the previous Saturn-Neptune conjunction of 1953 in the journal 'L'Yonne républicaine' (1 January 1953) when I wrote about the probability of a Soviet renewal. Three months later confirmation came with the unexpected death of Stalin.

> The fact that the Russian communist party came into being at the time of the 1881 conjunction and that they took power at the conjunction of 1917 leads you to think that the year 1953 will be very important for USSR. In fact the regime finds itself at the end of the cycle at the same time as the cycle is undergoing renewal; we can expect internal changes, perhaps a changeover in the Kremlin.

Now we can see the whole picture, in a triple jump, a historical thread passes through four stages (including 1989) in the transformation of Russia. This was followed by a new forecast in the 'Éditions Grasset' of 1955: *'A defence and demonstration of astrology'*: 'At the conjunction of 1953 Stalin died and USSR was in full transition; it began a new cycle which would take it to the very important completion date of 1989.' This forecast was made on many occasions and the last one, called 'The clouds hanging over 1989-90' was printed in *L'astrologue* no. 85 in the first trimester of 1989.

> Thus the only Jupiter-Saturn opposition from September 1989 to July 1990 is an indication of a critical turning point for the European community which will be directly involved in the new crisis, and will have to go through a major ordeal before reaching its historic completion date of 1992. Above all we have to bear in mind that Jupiter makes an opposition to Saturn-Neptune during this same period between September 1989 and July 1990. It could signify a time when revolutionary undercurrents surface with outpourings of popular feeling and people taking to the streets with the risk of governments being toppled. I imagine that there will be a possibility of such coups

d'état for the countries that are being suppressed such as Rumania, the countries of Eastern Europe kept in a straitjacket like Czechoslovakia'.

Cycle 1989-2026 : Nebulous policies

Now that the European Soviet empire had completely disintegrated and dishonoured the ideology that it was built on, the substitute formula of the new Community of Independent States (CIS) was hardly in a state to respond to the same cyclical phenomenon. Certainly traces of it appeared to survive; the Slavic soul may have some resonance with the collective atmosphere of the cycle. A semi-square (April to November 1994) occurred at the time of the first days of Boris Yeltsin who let the substitute state disintegrate into anarchy and corruption, the impropriety of a sort of historic abrogation. Then, at the time of the trine (June 2001-April 2002), the coming to power of Vladimir Putin was followed by a recovery. It's true that he was born on 7 October 1952 under a quadruple conjunction Sun-Mercury-Saturn-Neptune which contributed to him profiting personally as a substitution for lost power.

A more specific example was the exact correlation of the Saturn-Neptune opposition (August 2006-July 2007) which, with an orb of 3°, accompanied the crisis in France in November 2005. Here we had the cross of a Sun-Mars opposition at right angles to the Saturn-Neptune opposition. Certainly the Sun-Mars dissonance is a configuration specific to explosions of vitality, generally converted into those heated moments in history.

Well, in France on 27 October 2005 in Clichy-sous-Bois, a suburb of Paris, there was a sudden uprising of young people in the working class neighbourhoods which first spread to the provinces and then the big cities and a number of other countries, until a state of emergency was declared and a curfew established on 10 November. In the twenty days that shook France, with comparisons made with May 1968, these urban guerrillas left 7000 burnt-out cars in their wake as well as buses and public buildings destroyed and a great number of arrests.

An explosion of despair which led to a popular outburst, these demonstrations by a generation of young people from the disadvantaged districts of France were evidence of a revolutionary shift, a sign of the dangerous gulf between poverty and riches. Doubtless France had to be made especially aware of this shock; having failed to integrate the population of colonial immigrants who deserved better consideration. This makes us aware of the transit at the time of Pluto to the Saturn in Sagittarius in the 9th house of the Fifth Republic.

The following Saturn –Neptune square in 2015 merits attention, as well as the Uranus-Neptune semi-square which accompanies the Jupiter-Saturn-Pluto meet-up in 2020-2021, when there is a risk of more poverty.

The next conjunction in 2026 is centrally placed at the beginning of Aries and is in a triangular quartet of planets with a double sextile to a trine between Uranus in Gemini and Pluto in Aquarius.[11]

It is the most benefic configuration of the century and its interplanetary partnership will work for the best in a splendid relaunch of civilization. It contains a harmonious relationship between primordial polar opposites; the coming together of the external and the internal, rational and spiritual, mind and soul... human beings surpassing themselves while experiencing life on a higher level.

The contrast is striking with the following Saturn-Neptune conjunction in Gemini of 2061 which is square to Pluto in Pisces and sesquiquadrate to Uranus in Scorpio: a confrontation between warring brothers, promising great revolutionary storms. The continent of North America seems to be the region that is most exposed. This conjunction juxtaposes Mars, at 21° Gemini square to Neptune at 22° Virgo, of the astrological chart for the Independence of the US on 4 July 1776.

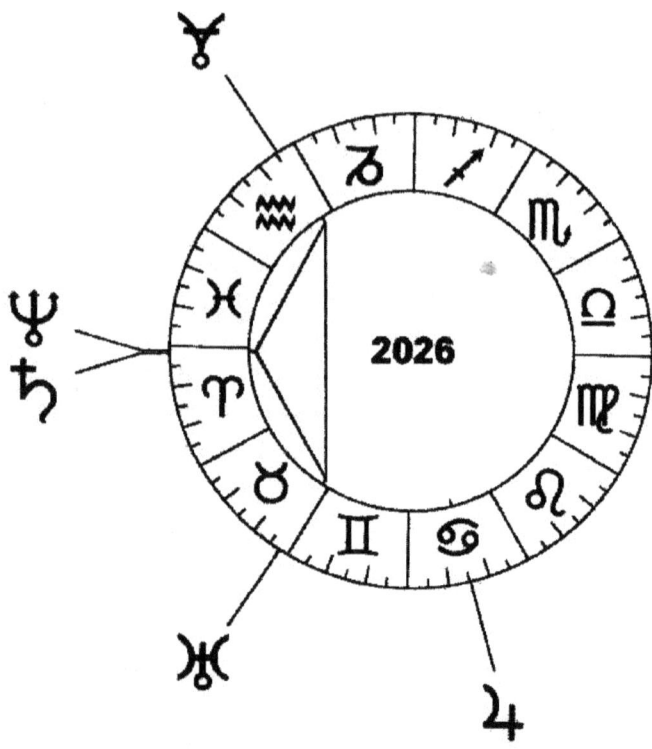

As a start, let us end the prejudices of detractors, and write large the predictive power of the astral signature to signal historical events and forecast what is to come.

Chapter 8 – The Saturn-Pluto Cycle

Taking into account the eccentricity of Pluto's orbit the return of the Saturn-Pluto conjunction varies markedly by a few years over thirty. In the 19th and 20th centuries there were conjunctions in 1819, 1851, 1883, 1914, 1947 and 1982.

We are naturally inclined to assign to this planetary combination a register that is dark and sinister, a double star that evokes the death wish of Thanatos. Its company after the Jupiter-Uranus conjunction in 1914 brings to mind the extremes of the German army's rapid advance on Paris to the infernal paralysis of the war in the trenches of soldiers who were bogged down. Besides the fire of the murderous artillery, there was the silent and obscene weapon of asphyxiating gases. But let's be careful of easy answers: each of these planets has just as many really positive qualities.

Pluto made a forceful entry into our modern society at the triple conjunction Saturn-Uranus-Pluto at the end of Aries and the beginning of Taurus around 1850. If the industrial revolution of the 19th century began at the Uranus-Neptune conjunction of 1820, it was given a 19th century. Certainly here it is difficult to judge the respective parts played by the participants. Nevertheless, the group exhibits a clear Saturn-Pluto specificity. In particular in Taurus with the unprecedented acquisition of new tools from earth resources: gold, metals, ores and coal torn from the bowels of the earth, already considerably valued. Chthonian resources having contributed immensely to the revival of the industrial revolution which in concert with the inventions of the Uranian technological genie founded our modern civilization.

The Saturn-Pluto conjunction of 1947
The conjunction of 1914 clearly contributed to the tragedy of the First World War. Following the lightning advance of the German offensive with its troops at the gates of Paris, the signature of the blazing Jupiter-Uranus conjunction, its role, the infernal immobilisation of the troops in the trenches, began: soldiers abandoned to the vagaries of the rain and the

cold, of the mud, reduced to dealing with vermin like lice and rats in total chaos and under threat of death. The Second World War had finished when the new Saturn-Pluto conjunction occurred on 23 August 1947 at 14° Leo. The consequences of this second world tragedy were just as heavy. Its manifestation shook the world; 1947 was the year of the great whirlwind throughout Asia, this continent rebuilding itself from top to bottom.[12]

Just before this, Chiang Kai Shek, sanctioned by a US treaty of protection and with a four million strong army, launched his 'final campaign' against the communist troops who had been driven out of a hundred cities, and forced to evacuate their capital Hunan. Then came a surprise military reversal and the victory of Mao Tse-Tung which led to the formation of the People's Republic of China on 1 October 1949.

At the same time, from 1946 to 1948, communist insurrections were triggered just about everywhere: the Philippines, Burma, Malaysia, North Korea and Indonesia. Also, when in December 1946, the communists went on the defensive in Hanoi, the first war in Indochina began which was to last seven years.

The heart of the matter was that the Far East was being decolonized with the clock being turned back to the beginning. The British gave up a part of their empire: India and Pakistan became independent on 15 August 1947 and this partition caused a war between these two countries over Kashmir in which 800,000 people died. Then in the west of this same continent Israel declared itself at war on 17 May 1948 and became a source of tension in the Middle-East.

Following the succession of aspects round the Saturn-Pluto cycle it's clear that this correlation is justified. Thus the semi-sextile fell at the time of the Sino-Soviet Treaty, the first semi-square at the Chinese intervention in the Korean War, the sextile at the fifth Quinquennial Plan (1951-55). In 1963 I was working on a major forecast about the opposition which was published in 1963 under the title *The Worldwide Crisis in 1965*

It is interesting to observe that the two great planetary oppositions of 1965-1966, because three planets are involved, are juxtaposed as if they have a common focus: when Uranus and Pluto are in conjunction, Saturn is in opposition to them both at the same time and in the same place. How can you not think that the American (Saturn-Uranus) problem and the Chinese (Saturn-Pluto) problem tend to blend into the same grouping. At the heart of the crisis beginning in 1965, we could have an explosive situation with these two partners, American and Chinese face to face (Russia finds itself marginalised in an intermediary position, a conciliator because (115) of Neptune's sextile and trine to the opposition). You could think then that the main concern/ critical issue in the tension between Washington and Peking. There is every reason to believe that India will be a player as well, like China alongside the Saturn-Pluto cycle. The independence of that country was announced in Delhi on August14th 1947 under a Sun-Saturn-Pluto conjunction. Since then the Saturn-Pluto opposition of 1965-1966 is also an important completion date for India and the two Saturn oppositions at this time symbolise a sort of crossroads where those concerned would be Washington, Peking and Delhi (...) A war or an operational front of a particular face is very possible; and with such a perspective Moscow will have a great role representing peace.

Well, the Vietnam War, in which the US engaged themselves in 1965 was soon considered to be a Sino-American war by the Vietnamese sides, quite apart from the effective participation of the Chinese supplying arms and men (in the 300,000's), North Vietnam being backed by their country's big brother. And it was the Soviets who settled the Indo-Pakistani war in Tashkent, India having been the theatre for the biggest Soviet entente at the same time as the biggest Sino-American confrontation except for Vietnam.

To better validate this provisional research I formulated another forecast in *The Planets and History*, Pauvert 1969:

> If the signification of these two forecasts is still under doubt, will not doubt and question both be replaced, if it is found

to confirm, as we believe, the indication for a Washington-Peking détente, in fact of a certain accord between the United States and China with this time the Saturn-Uranus and Saturn-Pluto trines of 1971-1972? (...) The crisis resolved itself; doubtless a Sino-American accord can be envisaged with the United States agreeing for example to retreat militarily and politically from South-East Asia and China, in this instance, giving way to the politics of peaceful coexistence.

Remember the diplomatic bombshell that astonished all the chancelleries at the meeting between Kissinger and Chou En-lai in July 1971, then the memorable handshake between Nixon and Mao in Peking in February 1972.

Following this Sino-American reconciliation, going back twenty years since passed on from the trines to the squares in the same cycle I took the risk of adding this time in *L'astrologue* no. 15 in the 3rd trimester of 1971:

> If one is not yet convinced to bet on one plausible correlation we can continue the experiment. After the times of the oppositions, the quincunxes and the trines there will be those of the squares. It's true that they will be much wider apart time-wise, the Saturn-Pluto square comes about in 1974 and the Saturn-Uranus square in 1976. We can therefore foresee for the period around 1975 that the Sino-American rapprochement will be erased if not cancelled.'

The euphoria of this ongoing reconciliation had to be followed, with the return of Kissinger to Peking in October 1975, by a confrontation over a variety of interests, to arrive at a normalization of relations in December 1978, this time under a harmonious sextile[13] Saturn-Uranus-Pluto.

Also in *The Planets and History*, (1967), and then at the time that Tokyo was much more important than Peking on the international stage, this is what I said on the subject of the next Saturn-Pluto conjunction of 1982:

> We have enough serious reasons to believe that the new Saturn-Pluto conjunction in 1982 chiefly concerns Communist China, the completion date for this end of cycle

taking on much more emphasis and brilliance because Jupiter is also there. Isn't it right to think that this may be a crucial stage for the new China? We have to think that at this point of renewal in the cycle China will become an international leader.

Without dramatic events for all that, it is since this turning point that this country has quietly taken an economic role, which could already be predominant in the world, Deng Xiaoping who came to power at the time of the waning sextile in 1977 converted his country into a liberal economy. Then around this dark triple conjunction of 1981-82 that the Chinese economic boom was felt all over the world. Finally, China, must she not become the world leader at the next Jupiter-Saturn-Pluto conjunction in 2020-21; especially as this will happen at the position of the Capricorn Jupiter in the chart for October 1 1949? In any case this was my projected completion date that I have repeated on numerous occasions over many decades. If not before, the cyclic transfer from Washington to Peking won't happen later than the next Saturn-Uranus conjunction in 2032.

But also, other countries resonate to the same cycle, and, just to cite one, take Israel (Tel-Aviv, 14 May 1948 with its trio Mars (28° Leo)-Saturn- Pluto (16° and 13° Leo) besides a Jupiter-Uranus opposition. Its most difficult times were at the dissonant aspects of the cycle: the Sinai War (29 October-3 November 1956) at the first square, Yom Kippur War (6-30 October 1973) at the second square and even under Sun-Pluto conjunction square to Saturn. And at the return of the conjunction on 4 June 1982 with this time a terrible intervention in Lebanon. It was natural that at the opposition of 1965 the PLO adversary made its appearance to take back part of its territory in order to arrange for a Palestinian State. However with a common inability to make peace it could only feed a branch of terrorism in the world.

There was another tragedy at the crossroads of the Jupiter-Saturn-Pluto line-up of 1981-82. It started with the fever of 20 November 1979 (Sun-Uranus in Scorpio square to Mars in Leo), the first day of the year 1400 in the Muslim calendar. That day one to two million Iranians demonstrated in front of the

American embassy in Tehran, where since the 4th they had been holding all the diplomatic personnel hostage in a climate that put them on a war footing with America. In addition the Great Mosque at Mecca was invaded by hundreds of armed insurgents who took it by force, shaking the throne of Saudi Arabia; while in Pakistan a crowd attacked and set fire to the United States' Embassy and at Medina other insurgents tried to seize the tomb of the prophet! The whole world was faced with the spectre of a holy war against the West with a people who comprised seven hundred million Muslims. With the Iranian Revolution as well, the departure of the Shah and the arrival of Ayatollah Khomeini in Iran, a new era began which would undermine western society.

Then less than two months after Mars at its perigee-perihelion direct station near the Saturn-Pluto ongoing opposition (from summer 2001 to summer 2002), we have the 11 September 2001 kamikaze attack that Bin Laden inflicted on the New York World Trade Centre[14]. This went on to launch the 'wonderful war' against terrorism, appropriate terminology for this aspect of the planetary couple.

This panoply of happenings does not mean at all that only evil and hate and other human barbarisms or deadly events are the privilege of or are exclusive to the Saturn-Pluto cycle. In ancient times did not humans employ just as monstrous deadly means as those which we see today? It is true that society is not alone and that nature herself is brimming with means of mistreating her guests without us being able to foresee from where a little worse will come.

It's enough to just glance at these natural perturbations and at epidemics in particular, thus in an exceptional stellium Saturn joined a Jupiter-Uranus-Pluto in 1347 when the most terrible pandemic in history occurred: the 'Black Death', decimating a third of Europeans in under two years.

I was especially discomforted when having looked at the projected tables for the planetary concentration of 1981-83, including the trinomial Jupiter-Saturn-Pluto, that I had invoked the spectre of a third world war, although I had preceded this threat in brackets every time with: 'For want of a pandemic or devastating invasion...'.

In fact, about the first fear I evoked I had just heard an authority from the Paris Academy of Medicine say publicly that from now on there would never be more epidemics to fear in the world. Thus I have to eliminate all risk from this side. As for a really devastating invasion similar to the fall of Rome or that of Constantinople, nothing imaginable of this order could be conceived of in our day on our civilized planet. Nevertheless, behind the scenes excessive immigration has come to our continent[15]. A natural exodus of poverty-stricken foreigners is search of a better life, beyond the nations' efforts to integrate them. Assimilation is a testing problem, because they live communally in poorly integrated overcrowding, to the point that European unity itself is being affected.

The coming of the triple conjunction Jupiter-Saturn-Pluto in 2020-2023, with a dissonant Uranus-Neptune semi-square as well, promises to be like a new constellation of general imbalance in society. Exactly what will happen is uncertain but the risk is generalized chaos.

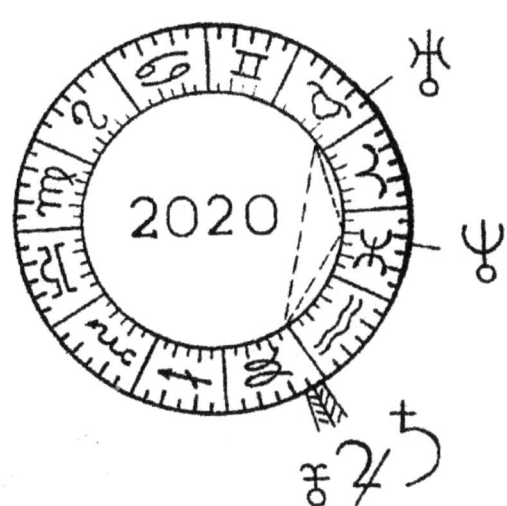

To return to the pandemic unwisely discounted medically, remember nevertheless that it was at the previous conjunction of the same astral trio in Scorpio 1982-83 that AIDS, a sexually transmitted disease, first appeared, with tens of millions of victims across the world, an affliction that became comparable to a world war.

Finally we have to go back to the first hypothesis of a third world war. If we have escaped such a disaster, don't we nevertheless have to remember that at the heart of the Jupiter-Uranus conjunction in 1983-84, besides the genocide in Cambodia, an Arab revolt in the Persian Gulf resulted in an undeclared war, seven oil tankers were bombarded and set on fire near the oil artery of the Strait of Hormuz with 239 Americans and 62 French (simple peace-keeping forces) victims of an attack in Beirut. Besides naturally the menace of putting euro-missiles in East Europe face to face with the Pershing-SS-20: a nuclear cataclysm narrowly avoided. Certainly terrorism hangs around like an endemic illness but it will be at this juncture that it will take on global proportions.

Chapter 9 - The Uranus-Neptune Cycle

The Uranus-Neptune cycle has duration of 171 years. We reach the next conjunction in Aquarius in 2165. In the years to this millennium we have experienced conjunctions in 1136 in Libra, 1307 and 1478 in Scorpio, 1649 in Sagittarius and the last two 1821 and 1993 in Capricorn.

In the solar system, except for the androgynous Mercury, the planets appear to be in complementary pairs: Venus and Mars, Jupiter and Saturn. Uranus and Neptune are complementary in contrasting ways: Fire-Water, compression-diffusion, intensity-dilution, uproar-silence, the individual-the collective... electricity and magnetism combined. On the one hand 'Man is his own Prometheus' (Michelet) and on the other: 'Every man has within himself the entire human condition' (Montaigne). So, 'There are two different ways of living your life: cultivating difference and deepening communion' André Malraux. The Uranian lightning which strikes from above combines with the Neptunian ocean that comes from the 'primordial soup'. And in politics you have these two extremes, that of totalitarian fascism 'one people, one Reich, one Führer' and that of Marxist collectivism with its rallying cry: 'Workers of the world, unite.'

First an issue that concerns these two planets: because they were once unknown, did these last two planets remain mute, as if they didn't exist, when we didn't know they were there? Alternatively, had they no astral language in the past? It seems reasonable to take a middle path: having always accompanied the group of seven, these two planets have always expressed themselves, quietly and then purposefully.

An example would be the quadruple conjunction Jupiter-Uranus-Neptune-Pluto around the year 574 BCE, which fell at a turning point in the history of humanity, with the advent of the philosophers and prophets who fashioned our spiritual lives, and introduced rationality and scientific ways that still dominate our thinking. As well as being the time that things are born, the conjunction is also a time of endings, and so between 431 and 403 BCE, the time of the catastrophe that brought about the downfall of the Athenians and the collapse of Hellenic society there was a cluster of the five slow planets around Uranus-Neptune-Pluto. Just as orthodox Christian civilization collapsed with the disastrous Bulgarian-Roman war in 976 (with the Jupiter-Uranus-Neptune conjunctions in 974 and Saturn-Pluto in 977).

There is no doubt, however, that the advent of the eyepiece [telescope] was a kind of birth for these planets that gave us access to their existential richness and at the same time augmented radical innovation. All in all, their discovery came at a time when there was an innovative explosion with the invention of the steam engine by James Watt; the balloon flight of the Montgolfier brothers; Benjamin Franklin's lightning rod; and the discovery of that miracle, electricity, the amazing source of energy and unlimited power which has radically changed life on earth. It's a fact that modern civilization was only established following the Uranus-Neptune coupling of 1821, which was at the beginning of corporate Capricorn.

But to go back to our predecessors; we have already had a brief overview of the Europe of Charlemagne, but only to dwell on the uneventful ordinary life of the time. In order to get to the Renaissance, we won't dwell on the conjunction of 1136 or on that of 1307 in Scorpio either.

Cycle 1478-1649: The astronomical supremacy of the children of the Sun

The following conjunction of 1478, positioned at the end of Scorpio and the beginning of Sagittarius, was particularly telling. This was when the Portuguese and Spanish navigators, like oceanic horse riders, made a giant leap forward with their caravels sailing up and down the shores of the African and Asiatic coasts discovering the unknown continents to the east and west. Christopher Columbus discovered America at this time (1492). These conquests were crucial: people had believed that they were on a flat expanse of the earth's surface and now they were learning about the

The Uranus-Neptune Cycle

size of the globe and its vast spherical expanse, which would soon be crossed by Magellan in the first voyage round the world (1519) just at the end of a Uranus-Neptune sextile which was not long after the Jupiter-Saturn-Neptune conjunction in Pisces of 1523. All this and, just as importantly [Gutenberg Bible (1454); printing started to spread the written word across the continent and minds were finally being woken by culture.[16]

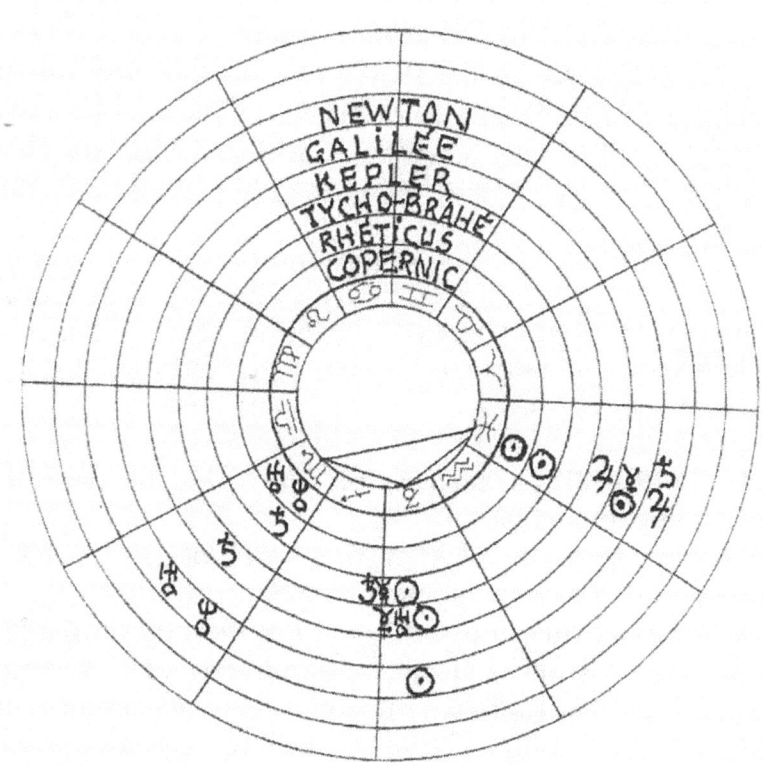

At the same time as this conquest of the earth's crust the cosmos was also being unveiled. This is a genealogical chart with the natal Suns of scholars respectively superimposed on a Capricorn-Pisces sextile (the foundation of infinity); Copernicus, Rheticus, Tycho Brahe, Kepler, Galileo and Newton; the team which led the odyssey towards the

Copernican revolution, the birth of modern astronomy. Starting with Nicolaus Copernicus, born on 19 February 1473, under the 1479 conjunction in Scorpio (13° orb), which trined his Sun, and ending with Isaac Newton (born 25 December 1642) with the same great conjunction (15° orb) with the 1649 conjunction superimposed on the previous one; also trine to the Sun. In addition Kepler's Saturn in Scorpio is placed between their conjunctions, Scorpio being the signature of mourning for an Earth deposed from its central place in the universe which it had held since antiquity, and the subsequent renunciation of Scripture.

In short, the world of communication was to give a new dimension to history. The cycle as a whole is also concerned with Europe's evolving future and we will start by concentrating on the Habsburgs who ruled over Spanish Europe.

The Uranus-Neptune opposition of 1563 came at a time that was more about division than creation. It was the beginning of the wars of religion between Protestants and Catholics which began with the Massacre of Vassy in 1562, and then that of Saint Bartholomew (1572).

Cycle 1649-1821: A succession of Spanish, French and English supremacies

The conjunction of 1649, at the heart of Sagittarius, was unusual in that it was opposed by a Saturn-Pluto conjunction. The same year this dissonant configuration accompanied the beheading of Charles I of England and also Cromwell's republic. Spanish Europe also saw a new beginning with the reign of the Habsburg Dynasty which was framed within in the cycle of 1479-1650, going from the unification of Spain with the merger of Castille and Aragon (1479) to the Treaty of Westphalia (1648). During the ascendant phase, 1650-1735 the redrawing of the maps benefitted France. On the descending slope of the cycle, from 1735 to the new conjunction of 1821, it was Great Britain's turn to be supreme.

The Uranus-Neptune opposition of 1734+ was right at the time of the Franco-English wars, at sea and in the colonies, with a succession of treaties: Vienna..., the peace Treaty of Aix-la-Chapelle (1748), though the war continued in America, with Great Britain maintaining her supremacy.

Cycle 1821-1993: The Industrial Revolution

When the cycle took root at the beginning of Capricorn a global society on another scale was being established, especially around the time of the Jupiter-Uranus-Neptune triptych of 1830. which boosted its intensity. This was the time of Romanticism with the liberating emancipation of the individual: inventions and technical innovations gave birth to an industrial revolution from whence emanated this [today's] unprecedented society.

Both the strength and speed of manual tools, used by mankind since the dawn of time, were supplanted by the power of the steam engine followed by the combustion engine, then hydroelectric energy. Just like Alexander the Great, Napoleon still had to travel on horseback and yet the first three locomotives were built between 1815 and 1817 and the first railway line (Liverpool to Manchester) opened in 1830. Steam navigation suddenly appeared on the oceans in 1819 and from 1838 ships with propellers crossed the Atlantic in 17 days. Between 1825 and 1830 the harvester arrived, looms for embroidery, sewing machines, the first electric motor and the first tape recorder in 1840. Everything followed: locomotives on railway lines revolutionized human travel, and the use of iron, cast iron and steel as well as the imminent extraction of coal and minerals gave birth to the great industries which, provided with new production methods, embraced the technical revolution which opened the door to individual initiative, the availability of credit and the markets.

Society had been completely transformed in two or three decades. Aristocrats and landlords were replaced by industrialists and merchants; all the power became concentrated in the world of the cartels and corporations that belonged to the big employers. Faced with a better life and the call of manual work, a mass exodus from the countryside led to a world in which workers concentrated around workshops, mills and large industrial centres. The urban transfer of the proletariat to the factories populated the sprawling cities.

The political birth of this new society came with the revolution of 1830 which empowered the business class in the countries where these great changes had already been made: United Kingdom, France and Belgium. Also in the United States Andrew Jackson, a self-made man, became president and so a symbol of the democratization of the American State. Conditions were now ripe for a confrontation between the social classes left and right.

Semi-square (1846-49): Revolutionary outburst of 1848. The first dissonance occurred when Saturn, intervening in the great cycle for the first time, became conjunct with Neptune. The strength of the opposition to the established regime surfaced: the Communist Manifesto was published just as the class struggle in France began with the revolutionary epidemic of February 1848, a revolution that was democratic and proletarian in Western Europe and nationalist in central and Eastern Europe. The repression of the workers' demands intensified in the retrograde atmosphere of the Holy Alliance which was reactionary in character.

Sextile (1853-57): A positive passage intensified by Jupiter's third intervention in the cycle from 1856 to 1858. A creative phase of real growth for a society that was developing at an uneven pace: the advent of machine tools of every sort deployed in all complex industries, coalmining, metallurgy and others... : delivery services, national rail networks, global freight and scheduled transport for international trade.

Square (1867-70), intensified by another aspect from Jupiter, dissonant this time, between 1869 and 1872: conflict and class war. Two wars in succession, Austro-Prussian and Franco-Prussian; the German State suddenly became a power at the heart of Europe, a new country, more conservative than democratic that went on to beat all records in the speed of its industrialization and to impose its laws on the continent. Meanwhile the class struggle became widespread with the First Communist International whose conferences fuelled the revolutionary climate (1866 to 1873). The Paris Commune (1871) was a poor attempt to seize power.

Trine (1879-83): With a harmonious aspect from Jupiter from 1881 to 1886 and a Saturn-Neptune conjunction in 1882. Europe and America were generally enjoying a boom; an atmosphere of peace and prosperity. Industrial innovation was at its height and the colonies were well established. There were agreements, cartels and international trusts (the era of Chamberlain, Ferry, Bismarck), subject to the constitution of the Triple Alliance bloc. There was some respite for both capital and labour because both were profiting. Moreover, socialism began to be and social legislation was put into effect; also more countries were adopting a parliamentary style of government and society was gradually being democratized.

Semi-square (1886-89): General malaise. The European States were shaken by internal crises. Notably, 1887 was the year when the continent experienced the worst tension since the Franco-Prussian War of 1870: Europe was a hairs breadth from a new war between these two countries (Boulangism) and from another, Austro-Russian, over Bulgaria.

Opposition (1906-11): Confrontations across the continent: Triple Alliance/Triple Entente, and the beginning of the Balkan War, which presaged the First World War.

This great turning point in history was fashioned by a complete cycle of Jupiter. In 1907 the Triple-Entente was formed (United Kingdom-France-Italy), under a Jupiter-Neptune conjunction. Europe was split into two blocs that were at loggerheads. By 1910-11 the Balkan States were at war. The great showdown erupted under the Jupiter-Uranus conjunction of 1914 and the First World War unfolded under a half cycle of Jupiter which went from a conjunction with Uranus, where it began, to the conjunction with Neptune in 1919. Also at this time, though not as tragic, the class war went through its final phase: clashes which started under the conjunction of 1907 with strikes, bloody First of May demonstrations and the Duma; all leading to the Russian Revolution of 1917.

Sesquiquadrate (1933): The Black Sea. This is a minor aspect but it is encased in a heavy Neptune-Pluto semi-square: three dissonances that together form a unique critical conformation. A goose-stepping Nazi Germany withdrew from the League of Nations and re-established compulsory national service; thus the arms race resumed.

Trine (1939-1942): From the German-Soviet pact to the Anglo-Americano-Soviet Agreement. The contrast is striking between this in-coming trine and the preceding out-going trine of 1880 when European society, on the back of its conquests, was flourishing due to peaceful colonization: the Triple Alliance and the colonial territories carved up diplomatically with the Act of Berlin. The Berlin-Moscow-Washington trio were now attacking each other. It's also significant that the outgoing Uranus-Neptune trine of 1940-1942 went from Taurus-Virgo to Gemini-Libra with an inversion of the rulers Venus-Mercury/ Mercury-Venus. Such was the process which operated with the chain of events beginning with the incredible German-Soviet pact of 1939, and followed by the partition of Poland, and then the Anglo-Americano-Soviet Agreement which came next in 1941-1942. Here the Neptunian 'communist' instigator, Moscow, interfered with the Uranian substitution of Anglo-American capitalism for Nazism.

Square (1956-58): There was open antagonism between the two powers that, during the trine, had been united in the fight against Nazi Germany. From the building war in Indochina and the aftermath of the Korean War, in which China was also implicated, the Cold War was in full swing. Also the decolonization of Morocco and Tunisia was in progress, as well as the war in Algeria.

Sextile (1965-68): 'Peaceful coexistence'. A change of tone: the 'Cold War' was followed by 'Peaceful coexistence'. First there was the international Moscow Atomic Treaty on 5 August 1963, which was then confirmed by a second about the demilitarisation of space,27 January 1967, as well as by a third, 1 July 1968, against nuclear proliferation.

Semi-square (1973-74): A real scare. The Yom Kippur War of October 1963 between Israel and Egypt which came at a time of extreme tension between Washington and

Moscow, while a coup d'état in Afghanistan was the starting point for dangerous Soviet expansionism all of which led to the confrontational placement of Euro missiles.

<u>Conjunction</u> (1990-95): The collapse of the Soviet Union. The fall of the Berlin Wall on 9 November 1989 promptly brought about the demise of the 'popular democracies' of Eastern Europe, and the collapse of the Soviet Union itself followed on 25 December 1991.

Cycle 1993-2165 : Globalization

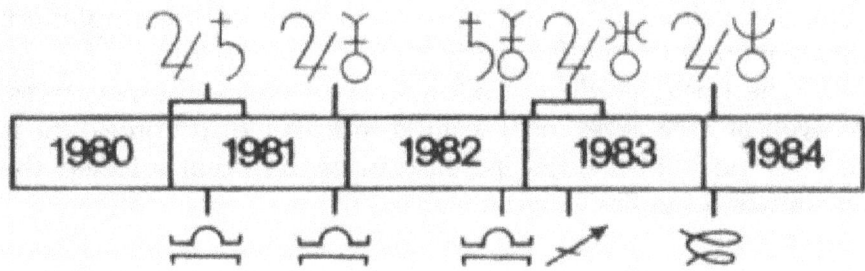

First of all there were five planetary conjunctions in succession between the years 1981 and 1984. This was the defining planetary concentration of the 20th century and the outcome was both positive and negative. On the one hand there were the Arab revolts that gave rise to a kind of rootless terrorism and also the outbreak of AIDS which decimated large populations across the world. On the other hand, it gave rise to a new culture with the boom in information technology, now well established with the universal use of mobile phones and personal computers.

The Uranus-Neptune-Pluto triad
This was the time that these three planets moved in close succession through Libra and then Scorpio. They found their agenda in what these signs represent; i.e. relationships and sex. Thus, when they passed over the first of the two, married life went through a testing time with a worldwide explosion in divorces and a preference for cohabitation. The next sign was crossed by Neptune (1957-71), Uranus (1975-81) and Pluto

(1981-95). It's not possible to imagine a greater sexual revolution than what actually occurred. Since the dawn of time the womb has always been a mysterious cavity. Look what has happened already. There has been a sexual revolution from contraception, with the 'pill' liberating women from the risk of pregnancy, as far as having the right to an abortion: ancestral bonds have been broken and you are your own person. This was followed by ultrasound, biopsies... The embryo could now be monitored: amniocentesis, fetoscopy, life in utero controlled until birth which is now without pain because of epidurals. And even, artificial insemination and fertilization *in vitro*, the 'primal scene' giving way to technical manipulation: surrogate mothers with a ready uterus, a womb to rent.

The positives do not altogether outweigh the negatives. As well as free love and the huge number of divorces, these years came with a huge increase in cancers that affected the reproductive organs of women.

Saturn-Uranus-Neptune triad: Islam

One of history's great beginnings was marked by a very particular conjunction that appeared in the sign of Virgo in the year 622. This Uranus-Neptune conjunction was joined by Saturn shortly after and was opposed by Jupiter in Pisces. No one can say that it went unnoticed, as is shown by this diagram of the birth of Islam the Hegira of 16 July 622. Moreover there is a concentration of fast-moving planets among the three slow ones and a crescent Moon rising.

This Saturn-Neptune conjunction spoke to a world that was searching for a new faith with an inescapable Saturnian rigour. And remarkably, this is the same triplicity that is repeated in 1990, this time in Capricorn and in trine to the former conjunction. At the time of this recurrence I came to the conclusion that this planetary return would signify a period of mourning, for us in the west, because *'it reflects an upheaval in the balance of global forces brought about by the new role played by people of colour, the old colonies, the under-developed, old methods...'* I envisaged a changeover or the elevation of the neglected and deprived of history, those who must take up the flame of destiny in their turn, superseding Marxist collectivism which had all but disappeared.

However, since this same planetary trio occurred again,[17] what emerged was a patent reawakening of the Islamic world which embraces more than 600 million people from Morocco to Indonesia and with some of this population having now been integrated, with more or less difficulty, into western life.

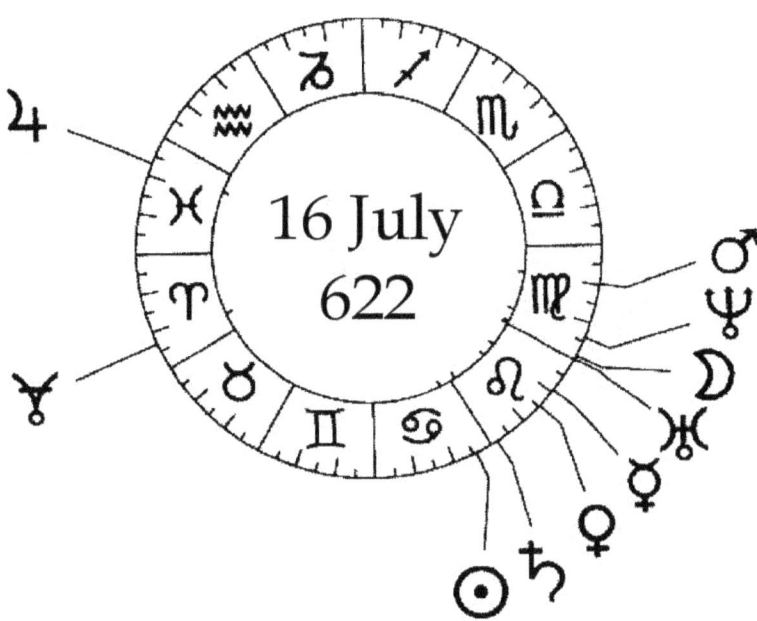

Chapter 10 – The Uranus-Pluto Cycle

Taking the eccentric orbit of the second of these planets as a given, all we need to know is that the average duration of the Uranus-Pluto cycle is 127 years and that there have been nine conjunctions over the course of the last millennium: in 948 in Cancer, 1090 in Aries, 1202 in Cancer, 1344 in Aries, 1456 in Leo, 1597 in Aries, 1710 in Leo, 1851 at the end of Aries/beginning of Taurus, then the last one in 1965 in Virgo.

It is not easy to formulate the igneous blend of Uranus-Pluto which results, symbolically, from a thunderbolt of lightning and the lava from a volcano; a mixture of Promethean ambition and new beginnings; the attitude of Janus with a multiplicity of resources. Here are the last two cycles which concern the demography of Europe and its profound transformation.

Saturn-Uranus-Pluto triad (1851): Global Europeanization
Under this triple conjunction, which fell at the beginning of Taurus,[18] the decade from 1850 to 1860 was characterized by a demographic shift which transformed the face of the world and inaugurated the Europeanisation of the globe.

To be precise, in the middle of the nineteenth century there was a sudden increase in the population of Europe with the birth rate rising by more than 30%, as well as there being a drop in mortality. The population of western Europe grew at the rate of a million a year during the course of this decade (a significant figure at that time).

This is how our continent became a huge hub for emigration beginning around 1850, reaching its height around 1854 and lasting the whole decade. This new phenomenon of continental migration mainly affected the United Kingdom, Germany and France, and ultimately resulted in the Europeanization of the globe.

This influx of immigrants indubitably established colonialism by mainly occupying the territories that had already been conquered: the East India Company with its trading posts dating from the earlier Uranus-Pluto conjunction of 1598; and the following one of 1711 when the English established their hegemony with their historical debut as the United Kingdom of Great Britain. They then established a doctrine on colonial matters, as well as the policies which resulted in the formation of the great British Empire. There was also a French presence in Africa. This meant that already in 1860, most parts of Africa were occupied by Westerners and this appropriation was completed during the last twenty years of the century. There were no parts of Asia either which escaped European contact, and Anglo-French and Russian infiltration reached as far as China.

The era of colonial conquest, with its expeditions, protectorates and annexations, was to dominate during the outward phase of the cycle, from the conjunction to the opposition of 1901-02. The last conquest of this type, the long and painful Boer War, fell in these years: this brutal colonization was complete. As well as this, xenophobia was on the rise in China (the Boxer Rebellion of 1900), weary of the conflagrations, lootings and massacres of its European occupiers.

During the return phase of the cycle, which began at the beginning of the 20th century and ended at the new conjunction in 1965, the situation in the colonies deteriorated. The increasingly problematic relationship between colonists and colonised resulted in the wars of decolonization. The end of the colonial era fell at the completion of the cycle and was the time of the settlement of the war in Indochina, the outbreak of war in Algeria, and similarly the intervention in Suez which tolled the [closing] bell for Franco-British supremacy in the Middle East. The Afro-Asiatic conference in Bandung (1955) marked the political birth of the people of colour in the Third World. At the turning point of the cycle, in 1960, when Uranus came within orb of the conjunction, about twenty states (the majority African) gained their independence. The great wheel of colonialism had turned full circle.

It is just as important to note that the industrial revolution was launched with the Uranus-Neptune conjunction (1821) in the earth sign of Capricorn and re-launched under the next earth sign Taurus, with Uranus (1851-58) and Pluto (185184) passing through the sign, as well as Neptune (1875-88). For this was the great era when man at last fully exploited the earth's resources, by tearing a wealth of energy-giving substances and minerals from the entrails of our planet. The world production of coal went from 90 to 125 million tonnes in the decade from 1850-60 alone, reaching 1000 million at the threshold of the next century. That same peak of 1850 was also the time of the gold rush: the world stocks of this precious metal grew by half in about fifteen years! While the giant oil fields were in operation from 1860.

And also, with the advent of modern agricultural tools—the return to oral [nutritional] Taurus—food began to be supplied on an industrial scale. In the United States the production of wheat doubled between 1870 and 1879 alone and at the same time farming became more productive with the intensive raising of livestock. This was also the time when—sublimated orality [nutrition]—property ownership boomed with land trusts and the inheritance of land. Money circulated as never before. Moreover, the rise of capitalism was aided, in the middle of the century, by the arrival of the banking establishments, the great shops and a construction boom. Fashionable neighbourhoods filled with large properties in cut stone, massive buildings with over-the-top facades; the triumph of materialism, of the market, of finance and the power of capital, in a word—Capitalism. A page was turned with the passage of the slow planets through Gemini and then Cancer. The world became less earthy and more refined in various ways.

Conjunction (1965-2021): The decline of the West

What was special about this new conjunction in Virgo in 1965, with its opposition from Saturn, was that it was an inverse replica with a reversal of what had happened since the beginning of the previous cycle. The birth rate in Europe now fell dramatically but, on the other hand, there was a huge influx of immigrants who had to be assimilated.

After 1964 the regular general decline in the birth rate affected all Western countries and the depopulation of Europe which continued over many decades became a major phenomenon. In post-war France, there was a recovery in the birth rate which varied between 800,000 and 850,000 a year. Yet, from 1964 the number began to go down and it went down as far as 736,000 in 1978. The curve had gone below 2 (2 children for each woman), the number below which a generation can't renew itself.

Yet this depopulation was a widespread phenomenon in a number of industrialized countries in the west: England and Wales, Belgium, France, Italy, Holland, Russia, even Canada as well. The birth rate began to fall in 1964 and reached its lowest point in 1980. In all these countries the birth rate then stabilized: from 2.90 children per woman in 1978 to 1.84 in France, 1.4 in Federal Germany and 1.5 in Switzerland.

Although mysterious in itself, there were psycho-sociological reasons for this demographic phenomenon because it resonated with the troubled economic climate. However, a more deep-seated cause can be attributed to the growing moral crisis which came to a head in 1968. This year, when Jupiter joined the Uranus-Pluto conjunction, the whole of western youth engaged in protest movements, and there was a libertarian reaction from women. The crossing of the conjugal sign of Libra by the independent Uranus (1968-74), followed by the baton being taken up by the predator Pluto (1971-83) set the tone. There had already been an unprecedented relaxation of moral values when Neptune crossed the erotic sign of Scorpio (1957-70). There was such a deep malaise that the divorce rate in Europe reached double figures during the fifteen years between 1960 and 1975. The birth rate fell as a consequence. Troubled adolescents naturally became confused and unstable, exposed as they were to the drugs which were suddenly everywhere. Their marginalization led to delinquency and even to terrorism which was omnipresent.

Finally, since decolonization, the movement was in the other direction in Europe during the last quarter of the century: this time it was the West which became the object of a migratory flux of people from the former colonies, with integration becoming a worrying problem. We can't exclude the possibility that the next Uranus-Pluto conjunction in 2104 will produce another large demographic change.

But our technological civilization will also be vulnerable, undermining the very notion of progress. The process of miniaturization that is specific to Virgo has given us the computer and a host of electronic devises that have changed our lives, but not without inspiring fear of the sorcerer's apprentice. Besides, we now fear the dangers of pollution: of the air, of water, of the earth, of our food... We have discovered the damage that has been done to nature, the limits of our resources and the enormity of the damage done by pollutants, irreparable for the existence of some animals. Out of this has come a saviour in the form of the Virgo-like ecology movement. Meanwhile, while we wait for the restorative resources, there is a heightened feeling of alarm as we confront the mess. In addition, as the eighties reached their height, modern industrial production moved its centre of gravity from the Atlantic region to the Pacific region. 'The decline of the West' was the theme of the work, *'The World Crisis of 1965'*

A Promethean trophy
When Pluto with its Thanatos-like powers is aligned with the promethean powers of Uranus there has to be the kind of progress that brings us the ultimate in technological achievements. Let's examine this premise.

In 1954-56, Jupiter passed by Uranus and then Pluto as they approached the conjunction. These were the years when the foundations were laid for the conquest of space. Completed during the International Geophysical Year of 1957-58, the preparations resulted in the launch of the first artificial satellites: Sputnik 1 and Explorer 1... Throughout a double Jupiterian cycle, Lunik, Venera and Mariner all followed in succession, revolutionizing our knowledge of the cosmos and giving us huge technological benefits.

And when the Jupiter-Uranus-Pluto trio came together, in a triple conjunction, man put foot on the Moon on 20 July 1969: the very day of the Jupiter-Uranus conjunction and

The Uranus-Pluto Cycle 129

when the Moon itself was crossing this trio. I had very naïvely given it a provisional mention in a work of 1964.

A technological revolution came on the scene with the Mercurian signature of Virgo which, faced with the infinite in the world of Pisces, was characterized by the miniscule, the infinitely small; and it was the quest for miniaturization that inspired this creative renewal that transformed equipment of all kinds: household appliances, industrial machinery. Electronics led the way with the first computers that came on the market in the middle of the decade 1960-70: enormous machines used for processing the typical problems found in industry, then used in the office. With the microprocessor (chip), miniaturisation became widespread and the end result was the sort of micro-computer we all use today which first appeared in the decade 1970-80. [*In 1980 André wrote*[19]] 'The cluster of five great conjunctions from 1981-1984: the computer will be in everyone's reach and panoply of electronic devices will be widely available: the mobile phone and its sequel while waiting for the Internet to be launched under the next Saturn-Uranus-Neptune conjunction in 1990. No doubt it will bring dramatic change.'

If we could make a reasonable promise regarding the future that has a good chance of being kept, it would be that there will be a new great phase of technological growth, altruistic in nature, between 2026 and 2028 when the outgoing Uranus-Pluto trine receives a beneficial double sextile from the central Saturn-Neptune conjunction.

The destiny of Japan
If post-imperial Western Europe emerged manifestly diminished from this great planetary turning point, other regions of the world became more valued.

This was exactly what happened with Japan which, according to historians, was founded in 1590 when Uranus was 20° away from its conjunction with Pluto in Aries. In any case the significance of this is that the history of modern Japan is fashioned on the 1851-1965 cycle.

The beginning was 1851-54 when this country, which had always been closed off from the world, opened its ports to western nations. The national revolution of 1868 took place at the sextile (1868-70): Meiji Mikado took power and modernise the country along European lines. At the square (1875-76), he imposed an imperial regime by crushing the feudal reactionaries. With the trine (1883-87), Japanese capitalism was established: this was the age of Meiji. Around the opposition (1899-1903), Japanese imperialism went from one war to another: against the Chinese (1894-95) and then the Russians (1904-05); at the trine (1921-23), the country became a great world power and, in a state of grace, it cooperated with the Western countries at the Washington Arms Conference (1922).

The following square (1932-33) marked the start of aggressive politics: in tune with a new Sino-Japanese war (1937) the Treaty of Washington was renounced and Japan withdrew from the League of Nations.

A surprising sextile – incoming – in the cycle (1942-43) was at the time of the Japanese military victories in the Second World War. But more importantly, when vanquished, the country became the beneficiary of the favours of the American victor, who soon treated it like a western partner. Potential recovery: they then faced the threat of the fearful Americano-Soviet Cold War.

Thus, with the return of the Uranus-Pluto conjunction in 1965, Japan went on to excel. It was one of the big surprises in the history of the decade 1960-70: the Japanese economy soared. Since 1965 innumerable technical products, *made in Japan*, have flooded the world markets to the point where at one time the futurists were putting this country at the head of the world economic powers.

You could think that this correlation, 'Japan - the Uranus-Pluto cycle', is dubious but it allowed me to make two successful forecasts. The first was exactly about the above: *'Could Japan have a spectacular revival in 1965-66?'*. An article I wrote in no. 99 of July-August 1962 of the review 'Les Cahiers astrologiques' was entitled: 'The historic crisis of 1965-1966'. The second dealt with the Uranus-Pluto square of 2010 and was in the 'special 21st century number' of *L'astrologue* (4th trimester 1990).

What I was to write about this dissonant aspect brought to light the following dilemma: *'...a social and political earthquake of high magnitude or an extreme crisis taking on the samurai-imperialist character of a pan-Nippon explosion.'*. It was literally an error but never-the-less it was a reasonable analogy, a symbolic substitution of something similar. The event which did correspond with the dissonance in question was the terrible atomic explosion in Japan on 11 March 2011 after a giant earthquake (8.9 on the Richter scale) and a tsunami which reached the nuclear reactors at Fukushima. In this case geophysics took the place of public affairs, and we are reminded that our configurations can't distinguish between a peculiarity of society or nature, and don't give us the means of excluding one or the other.

So, there'll be no surprise if Japan experiences a new era of full prosperity with the Uranus-Pluto trine at the end of the decade 2020-30, but then has major challenges at the opposition of 2036-37. However, once again, there is no telling at what level [social or material] it will manifest.

Chapter 11 - The Neptune-Pluto Cycle

This cycle, the last in the series (during which Pluto for at least part of its circuit crosses Neptune's orbit and enters the space between Uranus and Neptune,) encompasses a semi-millennium (an average duration of 494 years). Since the conjunction in 578 BCE there have been six. Four in Taurus: 578 BCE, 84 BCE, 412 and 906, then two in Gemini: 1399 and 1892. The next one will be in 2386.

The queens of inner darkness, the two planets that are furthest from the Sun, while being very different qualitatively, have in common that they are assimilated at the deepest level of the unconscious where the being has the least control and where there is no distinction between the best and the worst. So depending on the environment at the time the best we can say about this conjunction is that its effect will be nebulous.

Think of that early encounter in Taurus around 578 BCE when Uranus-Neptune-Pluto came together and were joined by Jupiter. This was the time our civilization was born with the advent of this 6th century BCE prophets (Zarathustra, Deutero-Isaiah, Buddha and Confucius) as well as Pythagoras, and the first rationalist thinkers. That's to say the advent of religions in the world and also the birth of human knowledge which gave us an appreciation of life. But there was also a [Neptune-Pluto] conjunction at the sacking of Bagdad by Tamburlaine, the Mongol cataclysm (1393-95). It is true that the greatest suffering experience by humans coincides with the greatest planetary concentrations and the ancients have dreaded these build-ups for a long time fearing the end of the world.[20]

We'll now move on to the last conjunction of 1891-1892 in Gemini which covered[21] the twenty-five years, more or less, from the end of the 19th century to the beginning of the 20th. At this time the human condition was undergoing a profound metamorphosis. Benefitting from the progress made throughout the whole ascendant phase of the Uranus-Neptune cycle, individuals at that time flourished under the reign of the generous and useful goddess of Reason. Science was at its pinnacle with a dizzying number of discoveries and sensational technical innovations; its prowess led human beings to believe they were on their way to becoming kings of the earth...And then, at this secular turning point, the blue skies were spoiled by a nebulous feeling of unease; the growing number of questions that came to be called a 'modern' or 'western crisis'. Just as Rationalism began to be universally accepted, the number of unknowns, instead of decreasing, had started to proliferate with the 'irrational' concept of the infinitely large as well as the infinitely small. This brought about huge transforming revisionist thought: Planck, Freud, Bergson, Einstein, Heisenberg, Husserl... It was like an earthquake that brings up unknown substances from the darkness below; the feeling that something had overtaken reason. The Impressionist movement was already expressing this mood, which also brought about a revival of esotericism and of initiatory knowledge including astrology. Equally, though it didn't happen to everybody, people experienced the hell of feeling disconnected from themselves.

This feeling became more and more general while the war of 1914 was to plunge the world into a hell without precedent, a total breakdown. Like the machine which ends up enslaving its employer, progress turned on mankind, whose engines of destruction were perfect for mass killings in the name of high principle. This is the diabolical infernal nature of Pluto-Thanatos. Where are the most elementary moral values: liberty, justice, rights, country, when humanity plunges into the chaos of massacres, blood, the degradation and debasement of mankind when reduced to a bestial state? Out of this, while there was an infinite number of acts of immense individual courage, came the retreat into bestiality, a savagery that was both individual and collective; an outbreak of perversions of every kind and the collective psychosis of a world that threatens, sooner or later, to use the ultimate weapon.

It's not surprising that the semi-square occurred at the beginning of 1930, the year when there were ten dissonant aspects between the five slow planets. This completely unstable configuration gave us the greatest economic crisis of the century, and on the back of that the rise of the brown plague of the Nazis. But we have to be thankful that, the orbit of Pluto now being the same distance from the Sun as that of Neptune, that a sextile between these two planets extended over the whole of the second half of the 20th century, something that could well have contributed to the 'glorious thirty' (1946-75 a time of great prosperity in France) and our escape from a third world war.

We also have to take account of the sign occupied by the conjunction then in Gemini. This first Mercurial sign is the signature of our society which is founded on the meaning of the sign, 'double' the duo, implying the notion of mobility, movement and exchange. According to the mélothésie[22] of Man-Zodiac of the ancients who divided the body lengthwise into the twelve signs, Gemini is the ruler of breath and the chest, the inhalation and expiration of air from the lungs, the dexterity of the upper limbs, such as the supreme digital exercise of surfing the web which has now become universal.

The Saturn-Uranus-Neptune triad
If the zodiacal headquarters of the Neptune-Pluto conjunction opened up an infinite number of possibilities for human mobility (think of the subterranean metro, a product of Pluto in Gemini at the beginning of the 20th century), that of the Saturn-Uranus-Neptune in Capricorn from 1989 to 1992 can only make you think that a fund of vital resources of a different order will emerge.

The contraction associated with the sign also could be seen immediately with the world becoming unipolar: the communist empire, which had taken shape seventy-five years previously and had been the most extensive on the globe, had come to an end and the US had become the only leader in a globalized world.

This sign is also associated with density. However, in the last decade of the century, spreading at lightning speed, apart from the invasion of the mobile phone, we've had the mad dash for computers and the opening of the Internet. Everyone is linked to whole world by email with information of all kinds being exchanged. After the telephone, the radio and then television we now have this ultimate means of communication (Gemini) and individual globalization is on the horizon. By the year 2000 the internet had been relayed to 150 million computers in the world!

The flip side of the coin is the reductive unification that globalization brings about, the whole earth taking on a dreary uniformity. Here we have the features special to Capricorn being expressed to the detriment of Cancer's values. This brings us back to the matrix principle, to the bubble of the maternal womb with its membranous frontier, being assimilated into the nest of the family, being inside the house, the home, even the clan. Collectively we find this when there is a return to nationalism, the patriotism of the mother-country which is sensitive to the lunar strata of the people, inclined towards the natural turning in on oneself. The situation brought about by a nationalist reaction (Saturn) and a refUSl to participate. In the spring of 2014, Europe was itself rejected by Europeans...

Furthermore, Cancerian mother-nature could find herself out of favour on other grounds; notably in the treatment of edible plants with genetically modified organisms (GMO), and, in any event, at a time of risky violations of a pharmaceutical nature.

The Jupiter-Uranus-Neptune triad
There as a triple conjunction in 1997, with Jupiter joining first Neptune at 27° Capricorn and then Uranus at 4° Aquarius. Globalization was still underway: after the Free Trade Agreement of the Americas (NAFTA), in 1995 the World Trade Organization (WTO) was set up to encourage economic partnerships and by 2001 had already involved 141 countries. Moreover, the explosion caused by the Internet changed society completely and non-governmental organizations

(NGO's) suddenly came on the scene for the first time in history.

The number of Internet host sites in the world quadrupled, going from 46 to 168 per 1000 inhabitants in North America and from 23 to 82 within the OECD (source: OECD). In addition, at the same time the number of mobile phones went through the roof, with telephones in China going from 6.6 million in 1990 to 87.4 million in 1998. In less than three decades the Internet went from being a small experimental network at the time of the Uranus-Pluto conjunction in 1965, serving a dozen research institutes in the United States, to a worldwide system with thous, nds of individual interconnected networks. Under the five conjunctions that took place between 1980 and 1984, computers became available to the public for the first time and by the end of the century there was an immense network covering the entire planet.

The world of the NGO's had arrived. Obviously these were not new, the oldest one being the Red Cross which was established under a Sun-Jupiter conjunction in Scorpio in 1863 but before this time, these societies stayed in their own corner or their own isolated sphere. Now some of these societies, because of the failure of the UN as well as other organizations, intended to participate in public life: a Neptunian vision in which those defending the interests of the collective make themselves heard. So in November 199,9 when the WTO met in Seattle under a Saturn-Uranus square, there were noisy demonstrations with NGO's making it clear that society didn't want ordinary people to be treated like commodities. Following this in January 2001, in Davos in Switzerland, a world economic forum met to discuss globalization and to consider how they would respond to the protests; then in Porto Alegre in Brazil when the meeting was about respecting the ecosystem as well as the rights and values of human beings, it spoke for the whole international community.

The year 1997 was also that of the Kyoto Protocol which called on the international community to deal with global warming, as well as being the year in which there was a watershed in genetics with the cloning of a sheep: Dolly was the clone of an adult animal. This was another revolution which transgressed Cancerian values. And after Dolly, there was Margaret, a calf which was cloned the following year: a historical turning point which could lead to the future treatment of genetic diseases or equally be misused by sorcerers' apprentices. Biotechnology, contrary to the nature of Cancerian values, successfully transferred genes between unrelated species, implanting, for example, those of a fish into a tomato or a strawberry. Transgenic agricultural products have now been launched whose value is debatable, another venture into the unknown. We also learned in 1999 that a normal cell can be genetically altered by a cancerous cell. The year 2000 was the year of the genome, with the prodigious international achievement of deciphering DNA. We also have the dawning of a new kind of energy, based on hydrogen.

While our world was being transformed by human genius, in the natural world, 1997 entered meteorological annals as the hottest year not only of the 20th century but even since monitoring began. The high temperature was put down to, aside from the Greenhouse Effect, the climatic anomaly of El Niño which brought exceptional disruption. Here the effect of the global concentration of carbon could come into play because, though it was thought that what we reaped in 1982-83 was the 'El Niño of the century', the 1997 edition surpassed it in intensity, as well as the peak being in December 1996 (when the planetary concentration was at a maximum).

Chapter 12 – The Solar Cycle

King Sun and his 6 planet sons, Leipzig 1714

Given that the importance of a configuration is proportional to the scale of its manifestation at a temporal level, it's natural that the five slow planets reign supreme over the future of the world. Nevertheless, the other members of this family belonging to the solar system also have a role to play in the calendar of annual and monthly cadences, and the Sun in particular has the powerful role of being history's midwife.

Remember the great call to arms of the European revolution in February 1848 which blew up so suddenly and spread to all countries in just two weeks, just as the Sun, with a dissonant aspect from Mars, passed into the orb of the Saturn-Neptune conjunction of that year. On 3 August 1914 from 1° to 8° of orb it was aligned, at the opposition, with the Jupiter-Uranus conjunction and formed a dissonant aspect to a Mars-Saturn square. It's worth following up these interventions by going over the various European crises that occurred during the last century: Moroccan 1905-06, Bosnian 1908-09, Agadir in 1911. It's edifying to look at one planetary encounter alone, because

The Solar Cycle 139

you can see that its conjunctions with the Uranus-Neptune-Pluto trio marked the Second World War. Phases.

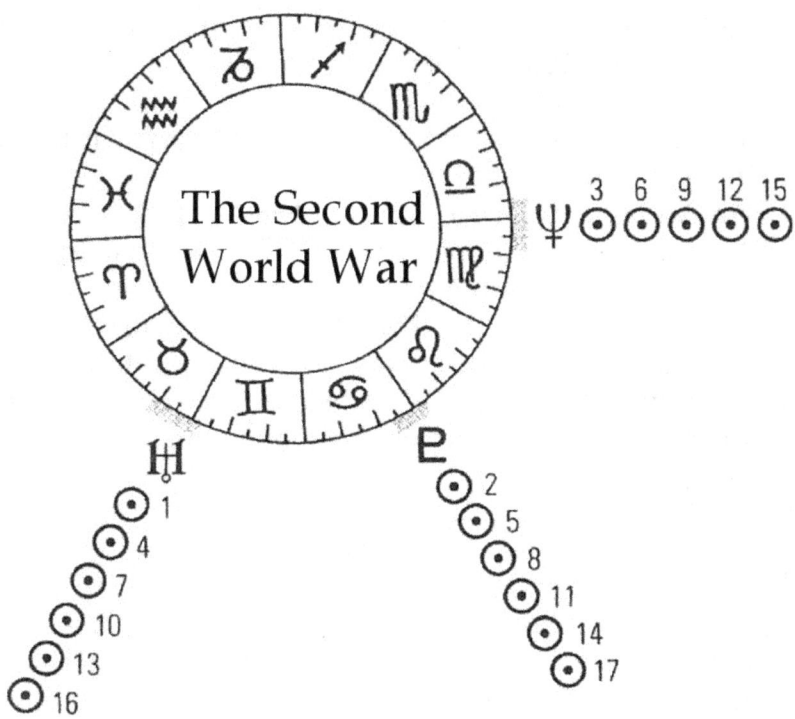

1. Sun-Uranus (12 May 1940): the final German offensive of 10 May against Luxemburg, Belgium and France.
2. Sun-Pluto (25 July): the beginning of August, the annexation of the Baltic States by the Soviet Union and the Japanese intervention in Indochina.
3. Sun-Neptune (18 September): 27 September, the signing of the tripartite pact between Germany, Italy and Japan.
4. Sun-Uranus (17 May 1941): 20 May, the lightening conquest of Crete, the German seizure of the Balkans and the heavy military mobilization in preparation for the offensive against the Soviet Union.
5. Sun-Pluto (26 July): 25 July, the freezing of Japanese holdings in the United States in response to the new war-mongering mood in Tokyo.

6. Sun-Neptune (20 September): 19-27 September , the tripartite conference in Moscow, Anglo-American military assistance for the USSR and Italy capitulates in Ethiopia.
7. Sun-Uranus (22 May 1942): 3-5 June, the naval battle of Midway, the balance of power in the Pacific tipping in favour of the United States.
8. Sun-Pluto (28 July): end of July, the Wehrmacht turns its attention to Stalingrad.
9. Sun-Neptune (23 September): the third week, the Red Army lays siege to the German forces in Stalingrad and Rommel pulls back for good in Africa.
10. Sun-Uranus (26 May 1943): conference of the Allies 'Trident' where the decision is made to land in France.
11. Sun-Pluto (30 July): fall of Mussolini. ON 1 August, Burma is given its independence by Japan and enters the war against the Allies.
12. Sun-Neptune (25 September): mid-September to the beginning of October, the lightening advance of the Red Army into Europe.
13. Sun-Uranus (30 May 1944): on 6 June, the Allied landings in Normandy, preceded, two days earlier, by the entrance of the Allies into Rome.
14. Sun-Pluto (31 July): 30 July, Americans break through the Normandy Front and bring about the liberation of France.
15. Sun-Neptune (27 September): 29 September, Dumbarton Oaks conference with the founding of the UN, and the Red Army enters the heart of Europe.
16. Sun-Uranus (4 June 1945): 5 June, declaration by the Allies ordering the occupation of Germany which had recently capitulated.
17. Sun-Pluto (2 August 2): 6-9 August, the dropping of the atomic bombs on Hiroshima and Nagasaki and August 8, the entrance of the USSR into the war against Japan brings about the capitulation of Japan, signed on 2 September with hostilities ending some time after that as the Sun approached a conjunction with Jupiter which was itself soon to be conjunct with Neptune.

While we are on the subject of the Second World War, I'd like to mention the role of the Sun in sealing the fate of armies at two stages in its cycle.

The war between Germany and the Soviets broke out in 22 June 1941 at the time that Neptune was in a T-square formation with the Sun and Mars – Germany's feverish preparations with a huge military build-up took place around the time of a great conjunction of Sun-Mercury-Venus-Jupiter plus Saturn-Uranus in Taurus (six planets within a span of about 10°!). A massive invasion that was successful during the ascendant phase, but at the opposition point when the Sun and Mercury opposed the three slow planets then there was a reversal. On 20 November the Wehrmacht launched a decisive offensive with the aim of taking Moscow. But on 1 December it was the Red Army that took the offensive and forced the German tide back several hundred miles, just as Rommel was also retreating in Africa. On 7 December the Japanese attack on Pearl Harbor joined this chorus of oppositions and the war became global.

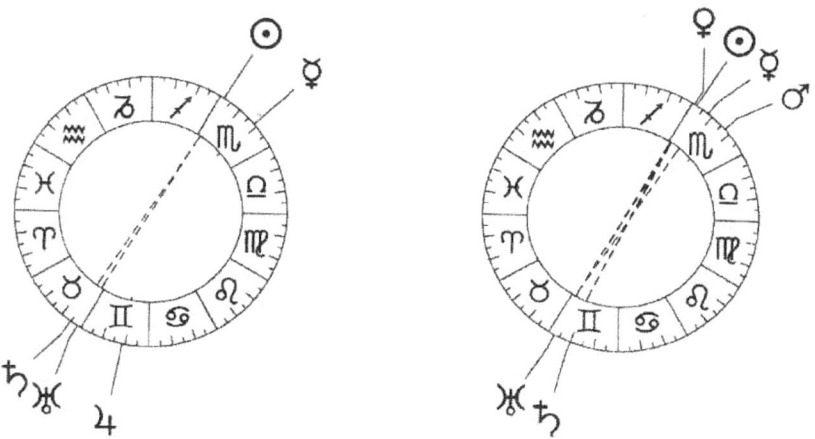

A similar process of cyclic reversal happened again the next year. In the autumn of 1942 the Führer set his sights on encircling the Red Army at Stalingrad. But on 21st November 21 it was his army under Von Paulus that was encircled and then lost after Von Manstein's army failed to relieve them. A decisive turning point, when the Nazi tide started to ebb, that happened when Sun-Mercury-Venus-Mars all crossed over the opposition point of the Uranus-Saturn conjunction.

This historic turnaround brings to mind the saying 'mandate of heaven', dear to the Asian magi: the power that the German forces had up to this point. A Saturno-Uranian power already shaken by the opposition in mid-November 1941, and which, after the Sun-Uranus conjunction on 22 May 1942 was transferred, and invested in the opposing power: the Anglo-American-Soviet Pact and the Japanese naval disaster of the Midway were also turning points, and the *coup de grâce* for the Germans was to come at Stalingrad, and then, even more so, with the Sun-Uranus conjunction in May the following year when the liberation of France began.

In the same way that this reversal had put the Third Reich on the defensive, at the following Sun-Uranus opposition at the beginning of December 1944 they had the advantage when they launched their last offensive in the Ardennes against an Allied army, which had arrived exhausted at the Rhine.

But the 'mandate of heaven' was for the Allies when the next Sun-Uranus conjunction on 30 May 1944 assisted the Normandy Landings, accomplished in one week, and they then went on to deliver France.

Chapter 13 – Cyclic Interference

While each configuration has its own individual features, its characteristics are shaped by the area of the solar system in which it participates. Nothing illustrates this better than a kinetic diagram which shows in a linear way all the intersections of the planetary circuits as they travel in their orbits.

We'll begin by looking at the Neptune-Pluto cycle, traversed by Saturn and Uranus. It starts with the conjunction, the centre of which goes horizontally along the two lines showing its chronological extension over the 20th century. We are immediately struck by the first transverse line that enters the domain of this great cycle. Saturn first appears when it forms a conjunction with Pluto in 1914 and then again with Neptune in 1917, and clearly this first crossing is aligned with the time period of the First World War.

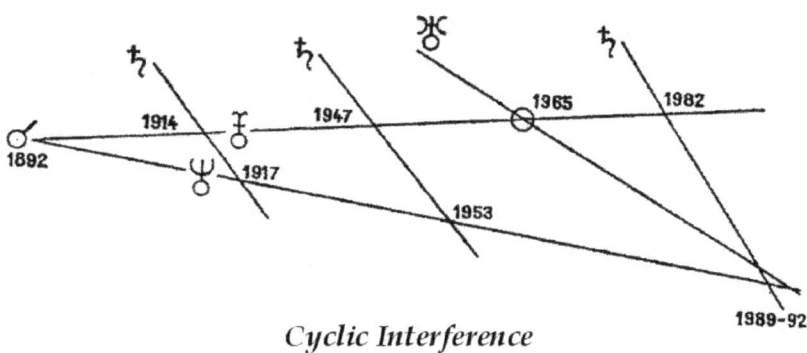

Cyclic Interference

The same phenomenon was repeated in the time period 1947 to 1953. This crossing was not as tragic but was equally radical. The Second World War was immediately followed by an era of generalized decolonization which began in 1947 with the painful liberation of India, divided by the creation of Pakistan, and then widened to a number of Asian states: Indochina, Indonesia... the movement spreading until it resulted in the Bandung Conference (1955). As for the third of

Saturn's incursions which began in 1982 and was greatly amplified by Jupiter making it a trio, it began in a climate of war with the Arab world in revolt, and ended by taking the shape of international terrorism. There was also the sudden arrival of AIDS, with its tens of millions of victims.

The intrusion of Uranus into the sphere of this super cycle in 1965 was even more instructive, with 1968-69 being the time of maximum intensity because of the triple Jupiter-Uranus-Pluto conjunction. It was the beginning of another world era. On the positive side there was the first man on the Moon, women's liberation and a revolution in information technology which brought about a new way of life; but we also have to include the youth crisis. Then we have a new historical crossing point which has three branches; this time the central round of the Uranus-Neptune cycle is aligned with the cycles of Saturn-Uranus and Saturn-Neptune, with all three cycles coming together in a triple conjunction from 1989 to 1992: an important point of convergence, a vital focal point which could only point to a completely new era.

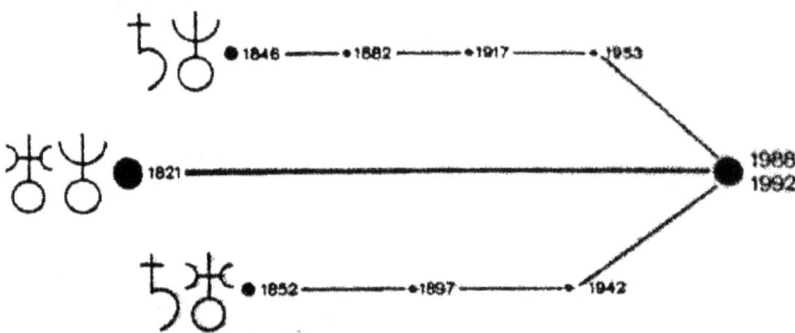

When one knows that the progress of the Uranus-Neptune [cycle] evolves in parallel to the ups and downs of our capitalist society in the same way that the cycles of Saturn-Uranus scan the characteristic times of the far right in our society: imperialist, totalitarian, fascist, in the same way that the cycles of Saturn-Neptune mirror the specific phases of the far left: syndicalist, socialist,

Cyclic Interference 145

communist, one can imagine that the fusion of these three cycles at the same time and in the same place could represent an important time of renewal in the real world.

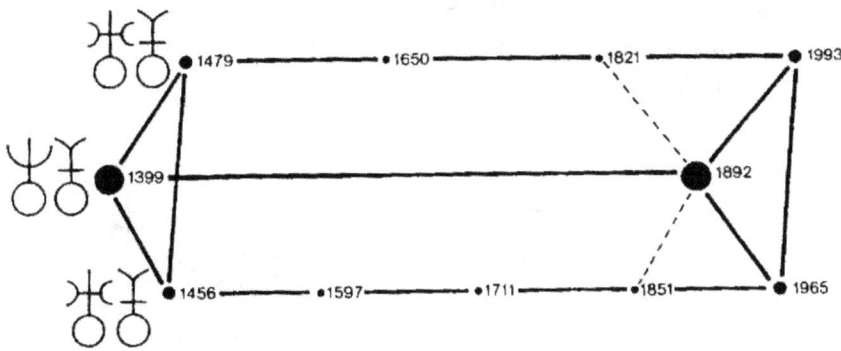

Having already decided that the best way of judging astrology was by making it speak, I began questioning this pantheon in the city of Urania when I was just a youth of twenty-five, and have spent forty-six years waiting and questioning this legendary distant realm which, when I was young, seemed a world away. My first act was to publish an article in the Parisian review 'Destiny' (no.16) in May 1947 about the historic path of the great Uranus-Neptune cycle which would end with the *'winter for capitalism'* and stretched from the square in 1953 to the conjunction in 1992 (the ephemerides at that time were not completely accurate). It concluded like this:

> We are coming at last to the end of the great cycle, with the conjunction of 1992 which presages a profound revolution in societies across the world between 1981 and 1997, but mainly in 1988-1989-1990, which is when Jupiter and Saturn cross this great conjunction. Will this be the end of capitalism,, will it be reformed or will there be a new regime? What is certain is that we are about to enter a new world.

The messenger is not important: what is interesting about the return to this article is that, half a century before, we were able to pinpoint when this watershed moment with its dizzying upheaval would be. What actually happened was, first and foremost, the collapse of the Soviet Empire and the curtain rising on humanity revolutionized by information technology and subject to globalization.

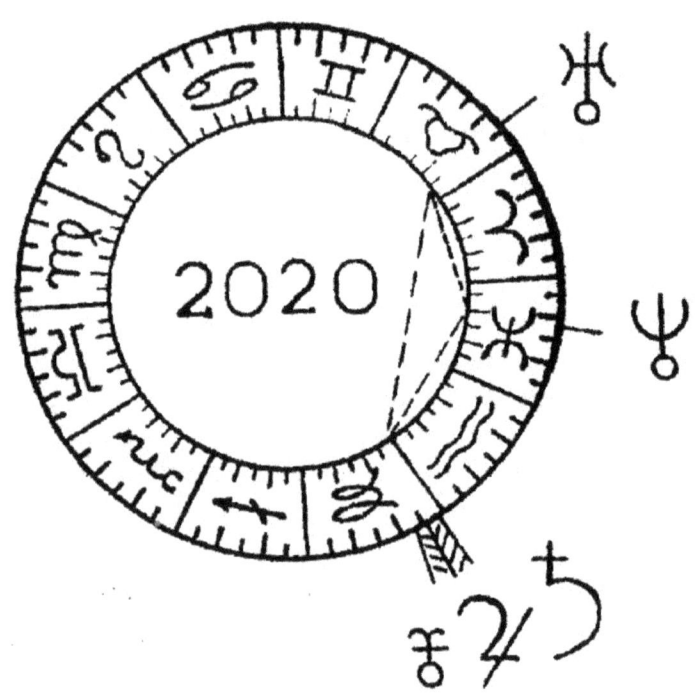

We have to look as well at the interferences at the critical next stage in 2020-2021-2022 where there will be a Jupiter-Saturn-Pluto trio squared by a Uranus-Neptune semi-square: a descent into world chaos with the risk of Europe being at the epicentre. There is another player that will affect these transits; an equally important factor that I will introduce later on.

With regard to the next critical stage, although its nature is unknown, you could think nevertheless that, if Europe is going to be particularly susceptible to this turn of events, it could be because the nation states here at home risk suffering the negative effects of globalization. Since this continent has become depopulated due to the fall in white births (1964-80), there has been an overpopulation of foreigners, with the total population reaching six billion. The migration of people within Europe, which people are struggling to accept, could get in the way of people naturally living together. In any case, the chaos indicated by the general dissonance may well not be societal and could just as well have a natural cause.

Chapter 14 – The Cyclic Indicator

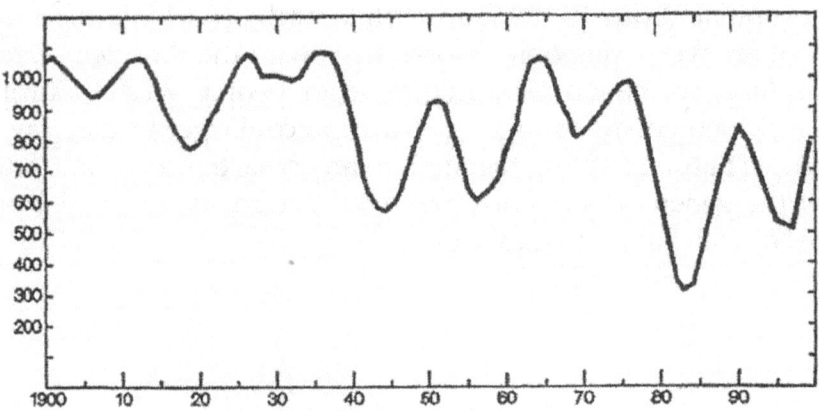

The subject of this indicator first came up in Paris in the 1930s when, in attempting to assess the risk of a second world war, Henri Gouchon came very near to achieving his aim. He calculated the zodiacal space between the five slow planets year by year, and was struck by how quickly he was able to state that contraction had been at a maximum between 1914 and 1918, as it would be again between 1941 and 1945. The observation led him to envisage that there would be no risk of a world war before the end of the decade.

I have followed on from this successful initiative, which was disregarded at the time, by emphasising the fundamental value of the cycles with their constructive ascendant and destructive descendent phases. Hence the 'cyclic indicator' is formulated using the sum of the respective distances (heliocentric, but that's not important) between these planets, the angular distances of the ten cycles combined. The diagram shows that the correlation between the indicator and the course of history, as shown here for the 20th century, is beyond doubt

Thus, the fall from 1911 to 1918 goes from the first cannon fire in the first Balkan War to the armistice of the First World War, which is at the bottom of the curve. The upward slope of the curve from 1919 to 1927 is the period of post-war reconstruction. The next dip from 1929 to 1933 falls on either side of the economic crisis of the century, which flared up in

1929 and reached its worst point in 1933. The great fall from 1936 to 1945 goes from Hitler's first offensives, the new wars in Ethiopia, Spain and Manchuria, to the armistice of the Second World War at the bottom of the curve. More post-war reconstruction as the curve rises from 1945 to 1950. Another fall in 1950 with the Korean War which marked the start of the Cold War, followed by the war in Algeria, the point at which it drops falling on the Soviet intervention in Hungary and the failed expedition in Suez. While the greatest rise of the indicator for that century (1956-64) was at the time of expansionist euphoria in the sixties.

The downward turn of the curve in 1965 was at the time of the American military engagement in Vietnam and its lowest point falls in 1968: the Soviet intervention in Czechoslovakia and the revolt of youth worldwide. A further drop in 1975 falls at beginning of a new economic crisis and a return to the Cold War until it reaches the bottom of the wave in 1982-3: on the verge of a third world war with a widespread recession and thirty-one million unemployed, according to the OECD, plus the coming of AIDS. With the rise of the indicator there is both a return to expansion and an East-West rapprochement which results in the end of the Cold War. There is a change of course at the indicator's high point of 1990 with the taking down of the Berlin Wall, as well as the collapse of the popular democracies, as well as another Gulf crisis and the disintegration of societies across the world up until the last years of the century.[23]

We have to take this diagram into consideration. However, in addition to the shape of the graph which shows the ebb and flow of this indicator, we must also take account of how far it rises and falls, the intensity of its message.

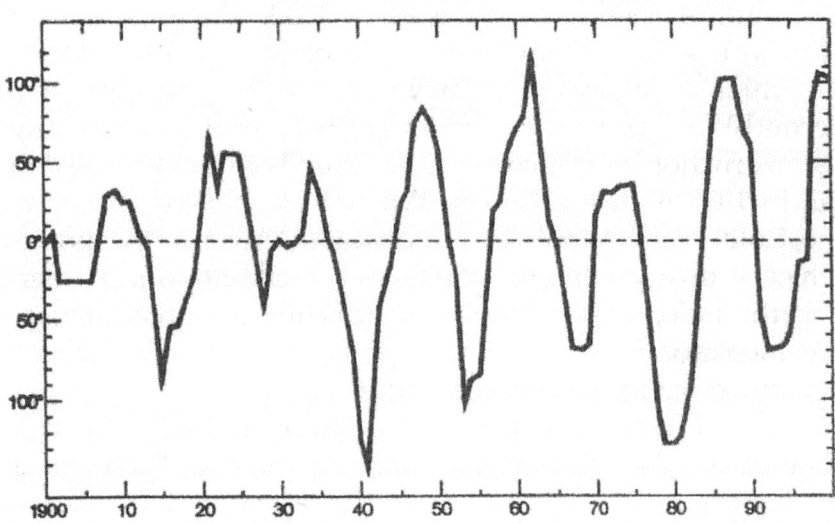

Thus, the same indicator went up 3° in 1900 (from 1066° to 1069°) and fell by 25° in 1901 (1069° to 1044°)... However, in this new diagram the indicator for 1914 shows a fall of 90° (1001°-910°). Another rapid fall can be observed next in 1927 (-57°): the tumultuous economic boom which presaged the Great Depression.

Then comes a record for the cycle in 1940, which inaugurates the Second World War, the indicator falling by 143°! Next we come to 1952: the Korean War and nuclear madness, and 1966-67: the Chinese Cultural Revolution, followed by student revolts in twenty-six countries. Then again 1978-80: the great oil shock and a world economic crisis in a climate of war: Afghanistan, Poland, Iran, Iraq... And conversely, the three principal peaks at better times 1959-62, years of great prosperity, opulence and economic growth then 1989 with the fall of the Berlin Wall as well as the amazing spread of the Internet between 1999-2000.

Coming to the indicators for the 21st century in the top diagram of the interplanetary distances overleaf, we can see that the first low point is in 2010, which justifies the forecast of an economic crisis perceived two decades earlier. And one can only wonder about the extreme depth of the trough as the wave plunges in 2020-21, the result of the next Jupiter-Saturn-Pluto triptych which will be relatively close to Uranus and Neptune.

It seems that Europe will be at the epicentre of this dissonance, either compelled to reform itself or threatened with division because its space is limited. At least, that's if there are no natural disasters or a new pandemic, which would be suitable substitutes. In any case it will be a time of widespread discord.

The second diagram is impressive, with the great swing of the pendulum from the lowest to the highest point between 2018 and the peak of 2026 where here, conversely, there is a harmonic Saturn-Neptune conjunction at the central point of an encouraging double sextile to Uranus and Pluto which are trine to each other It will probably be a change for the better when the headlines will be more agreeable and the civilization of our new mini Great Year at last becomes adult.

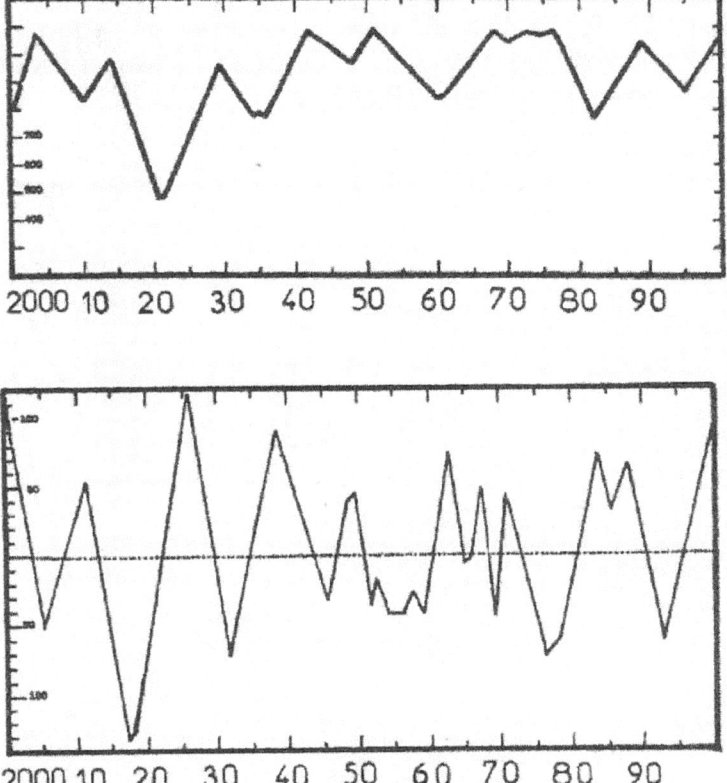

Together with the present course of the Uranus-Neptune cycle, we have a complete picture of the general evolution of the new century and, in spite of the general curve engaging with the ascendant phase, before promising a bright future we need to take a look at the impressive peak of 2080-81, when a Jupiter-Saturn conjunction passes over a Uranus-Neptune opposition: a kind of intensification of 1914 and 1942. This is undoubtedly a critical juncture with an extreme planetary threat. Useless to try and probe the mystery of this disturbing configuration that is so far off when we don't know if the threat is human or natural or both.

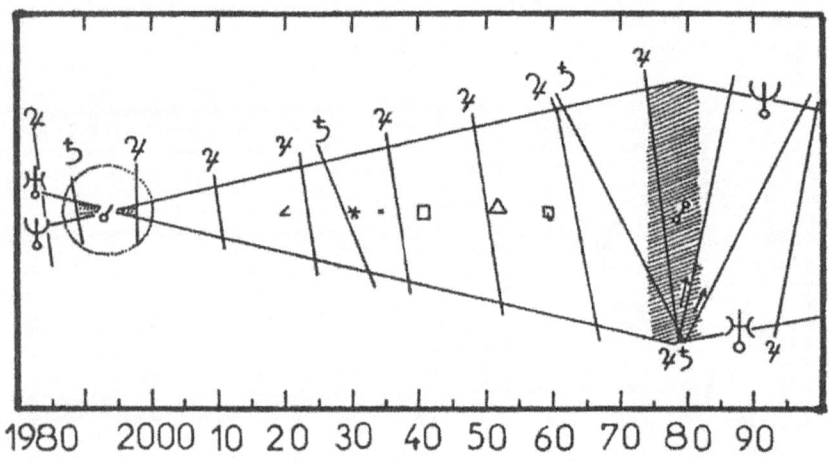

Chapter 15 – Astral Alignments

The planetary cycles completely encompass the evolution of the world, but nevertheless their paths do not cover the domain of the localized configurations which manifest in a rewarding way and have the value of supplementing our historical knowledge, particularly by looking at the planetary alignments.

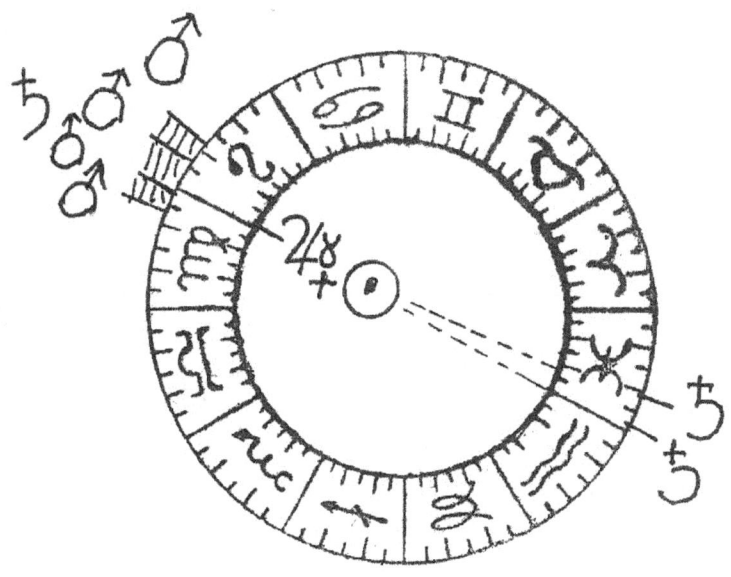

A spectacular illustration, which concerns one individual, is the beheading of the king of France, Louis XVI (born Versailles, 23/8/1754; 06.25; *Mercure de France,* October 1754), on 21 January 1793 in a public square in Paris.

This man was born under a magisterial Sun-Mercury-Jupiter conjunction at 29° Leo just above the Ascendant. There was nothing predestined about his wearing the royal crown because his grandfather Louis XV had many successors ahead of him. However, as happens when a culmination of Jupiter gives the throne to the younger brother over the head of the elder,[24] it was to him that the royal sceptre fell in the distressing climate of a conjunction in the 12th house. This was someone who was also the victim of a Grand Cross between Uranus on the Descendant, Pluto on the IC, the MC and the Ascendant with Mars conjunct.

The four leaders, who personified the fanatical French Revolution, were to rain down in concert on this dissonance. Danton (26/10/1759), Robespierre (6/05/1758), Marat (24/05/1743), Saint-Just (25/08/1767). By the concentration of their Mars on this royal triple conjunction! Thus Robespierre's Mars (17° Leo), Danton's (23° Leo), then Marat's (1° Virgo) and Saint-Just's (6° Virgo) were massed around the royal astral trio. And at the height of the revolution there were as many as three Mars-Neptune conjunctions which came into play with Robespierre, Danton and Saint-Just. They were then joined by the Saturn oppositions of Robespierre (2° Pisces) and Danton (11° Pisces). As for Marat, he had a Mars-Saturn conjunction at 0°-1° Virgo, while Saint-Just had a stellium composed of Sun-Mercury-Neptune-Mars, at 1° to 6° Virgo! Such a concentration of interventions puts you in fear of the worst kind of danger. The same tragedy which was to happen to the executioners in their turn.

But when it comes to warlike behaviour you also have to view the collective roll in any potential aggression as if it was the effect of a contagion and an example would be the European wars of the French Revolution and the Empire. The most significant thing, here, is the Martian alignment of the characters involved, just as if they were on parade at a military ceremony. Thus with his Mars-Ascendant, the debonair Louis XVI opened the ball[25] on 20 April 1792 by declaring war on Austria, with the secret hope of sabotaging the revolution.

On the other side, Francis II of Habsburg (born Florence, 12/2/1768; 04.30), nephew of Marie Antoinette and father of Marie-Louise, made three declarations of war: again Mars on the Ascendant. Then it was the turn of Prussia with Frederic William III (born Potsdam 3/8/1770; 06.00) Mars on the MC; and of his wife, the bellicose Queen Louise (10/3/1776; 07.00): Mars conjunct the Ascendant and the Sun. Then we have Russia with first, Paul I (born St. Petersburg, 1/10/1754; 12.30): Mars on the MC, followed by Alexander I (born Saint-Petersburg, 23/12/1777; 11.00): Mars on the Ascendant. Lastly, Great Britain with George III: Mars in Aries on the MC! The Martian picture is now complete and we can smell the gunpowder

Being able to throw light on such enigmas is invaluable and as well as studying the personalities involved by comparing whether they have affinities or antagonisms, you can also look at the national institutions engaged in such international ventures. Take just two historical aspects of the Second World War.

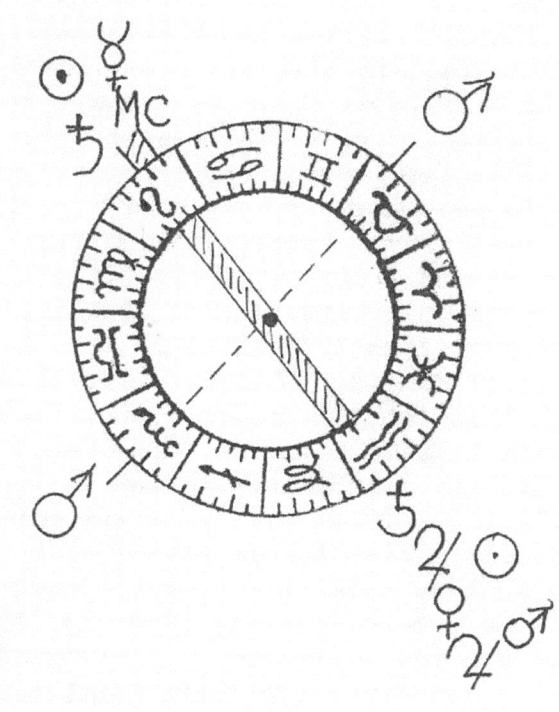

First, the plethora of principal players in this tragedy. Nothing is more striking than this diagram of the Second

World War which I examined in my work of that name. It's the hawkish tone of the opposition crossed by the alignment of the two planetary clusters which are face to face which jumps out at you. On one side, the duo of Hitler's MC-Saturn and Mussolini's Sun-Mercury in Leo; and on the other a concentration of six positions in Aquarius: the Saturn of Churchill, the Jupiter of Stalin, the Sun-Venus conjunction of Roosevelt and the Mars-Jupiter conjunction of de Gaulle. With, in addition, Hitler's Mars in Taurus opposing Stalin's Mars in Scorpio, their respective positions classed traditionally as being in detriment (exiled) and dignity (enthroned).

Next there are the circumstances of the principal countries involved in this tragedy. This second diagram shows the positions for Mars for the main antagonists: France (Third Republic, 4/9/1870) 27° Cancer; England (monarchy, 25/12/1066) 8° Aquarius; USSR (took power, 7/11/1917) 2° Virgo; US (4/7/1776) 21° Gemini; Germany (Third Reich, 30/1/1933) 19° Virgo; Italy (30/10/1922) 29° Capricorn ; Japan (monarchy, 11/2/1889) 25° Pisces.

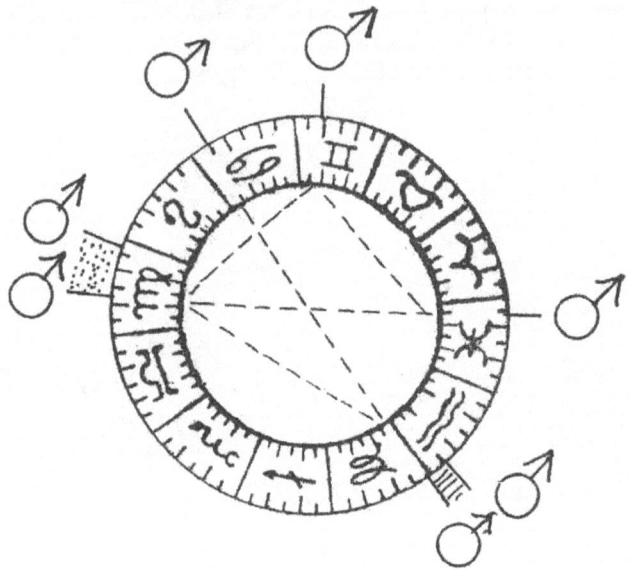

Some more input: war broke out in the summer of 1939 when

Pluto was transiting the Mars-Uranus conjunction on the Descenant of the Third French Republic at 25°-27° Cancer, at the same time that Neptune was transiting the Mars of the Third Reich, and there was also a perihelic Sun-Mars opposition – when the planet closest to the Earth – on 23 July 23 1939 at 29° Capricorn. Moreover, the Sun-Mars opposition was aligned with the Mars for England, France and Italy.

The Germanic Mars is almost conjunct the Soviet Mars in the same sign, aligned with that of Japan while making dissonant aspects to those of London and Washington. As for the latter, torn every which way in a T-square with Berlin's Mars and that of Tokyo, there's no better way to condemn a country to fighting on two fronts. Thus, this resource is part of the additional information needed for a complete overview of history.

The Epicycles of Mars
These have been an important indicator and could be most relevant in the 21 Century.[26]

This diagram shows the movement of Mars in relation to the Earth between 1927 and 1942. We can see a rosette of seven loops, or epicycles, round the central circle which represent the incursions of the red planet into the Earth's zone. The planet is nearest to the Earth when at opposition to the Sun. When Mars is at perigee (the point in its orbit when it is closest to the Earth), at the same time that it is at perihelion (when its orbit comes closest to the Sun), this is a perihelic opposition which usually happens every fifteen years. This is when Mars is closest to us. We can see that this is what happened in August 1939 – one of the signs that war would break out in Europe – then in October 1941 when Japan was planning its attack on Pearl Harbor which would globalise the war. A perihelic opposition of Mars also occurred in the summer of 2001, a few weeks away from the kamikaze attack in New York on 11 September of that year.

We are now approaching the next Martian epicycle: Mars will be at perihelion from 22 May 2016 when the proximity of the planet from our globe will be 47 million miles. With a Sun-Mars opposition which is semi-square and sesquiquadrate to Pluto, followed by the passage of a Sun-Venus conjunction in opposition to Saturn in a T-square with Neptune in the first ten days of June.

There is reason to fear a natural disaster, if not a world catastrophe, especially with the cyclic indicator crossing the sign of its detriment.

Chapter 16 – The Great Year

At the end of our exploration of mundane astrology, let's return to the multiple interconnected planetary cycles that go from one half-millennium to the next in the micro Great Year. This occurred on a small scale with the last trio which consisted of the central Neptune-Pluto cycle (1399-1892) framed by the three Uranus-Neptune cycles (1479-1650-1821-1993) and four Uranus-Pluto cycles (1455-1597-1710-1851-1965).

Going back to the time of the triple Uranus-Neptune-Pluto conjunction in the second half of the 6th century BCE (around 574 BCE), a turning point in history which was the era in which our civilization had its beginnings with the appearance of several religions as well as the dawn of rational thought. Later this convergence of the three planets accompanied the disappearance of the Roman civilization and the start of the Middle Ages and a double millennium. Then came the Renaissance in a triangle going from the advent of printing to the discovery of America. And the later date was when the world was being a Europeanized under the auspices of the 'civilization of western Christianity'. The micro Great Year ended at the end of the 20th century.

Remember that the idea of the Great Year came from the Chaldeans and Hindus and was passed down to the early Church Fathers, via Pythagoras, Plato, Aristotle, the Stoics and Neo-Platonists. Is it just an archetype that only has symbolic value? Astronomers and astrophysicists have been curious about it for a long time and are interested in the principle which is a fundamental, even monumental, geophysical resource.

So, let's hold with it, and its dozens of interpretations, the tenth movement of the Earth as our globe is subjected to the perturbations that are caused by the way the giant planets are distributed around the Sun. When the planets are well spaced, the centre of the planetary orbits is roughly juxtaposed with the heart of the Sun giving them all a common centre. Conversely when they are grouped together, in a cluster on the same side, this concentration distances their two central points and causes a state of imbalance.

This can be seen in the diagram overleaf, which is taken from Camille Flammarion's *Popular Astronomy*, and shows the arabesque-like movements of the phenomenon between 1910 and 1953. Looking at this ballet of the relationship between the planetary centre and the centre of the Sun, you can see that the extreme displacements of the two central points really stand out and cover, approximately, the period of the two great world wars! Can these geophysical deviations, which are a summary of the cyclic index, be no more than a harmless drawing? Isn't what we have here some inviting new material in the art of Urania?

We are now at the end of this overview of history. It's not been possible to avoid repeating a lot of the subject matter but it's a good idea to see the major turning points from all angles in order to see the whole picture. Even with these tools we are still feeling our way, blindly, when we approach the future in this way. Urania has not said her last word and it's by perfecting her art that we will have the best possible understanding of what is to come.

The Great Year

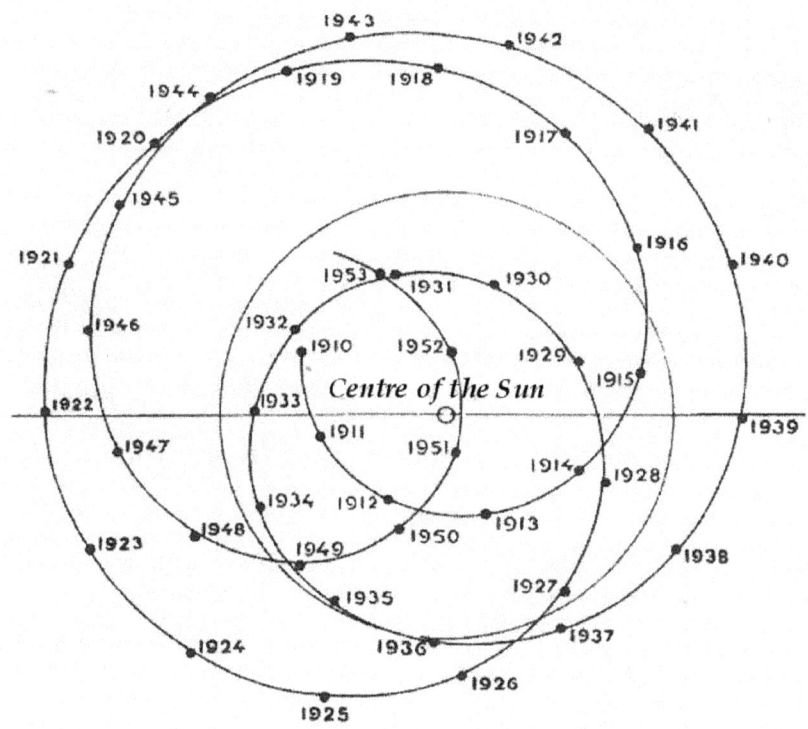

Chapter 17 - Conclusion

Finally, in this exploration of planetary cycles and their relationship with history, it seems to me that the brazen rejection of astrology is daringly audacious. It is true that 'it's harder to crack a prejudice than an atom' (Einstein)... But blind denial has to end: all the evidence points to the astral message being recognized. Moreover, it must be increasingly difficult to just shut one's eyes. We have to return to the approach of that giant, Laplace:

> An intelligence which, at a given moment, would know all the forces which animate nature and the respective positions of the beings from which it is composed, if incidentally it were vast enough to submit this data to analysis, it would include in the same formula the movements of the greatest bodies in the universe and those of the lightest atoms: nothing would be uncertain, and it would see the future, as it sees the past.[27]

While we wait, please excuse what could appear to be exhibitionism in citing my own success in forecasting, but I couldn't avoid it when the end result was this welcome gem of as yet unpublished knowledge. We have to look to the open sky to attain this precious goal of truth and the tribunal of time will give its verdict. Besides, don't we have to go on forecasting the future so that finally we can give Dame Urania a respectful bow?

Paris, June 2014.

Editor's Notes

Editor's Preface
[1] What distinguishes André from lesser 'cherry picking' astrologers.
[2] André Barbault, *The Value of Astrology,* page 122. [Pub. 2014. The A.A.]

Chapter 2
[3] In the original French André refers to a "London Pact" as being crucial in achieving this, whereas most authorities refer to the 5th September as the date of the First Battle of the Marne, which was critical in defending Paris. We have amended the text accordingly.

Chapter 3
[4] Hitler has Saturn in the 10th house, Himmler's Saturn near the MC when using the 16.28 birth time and Goering Saturn in the 10th. The mid-day chart for 30 January 1933 Berlin, when Hitler took over the Reichstag also has Saturn very close to the MC. Birth data: Hitler 20 April 1889, 18.30, Braunau am Inn, Austria; Goering, 12 January1893, 04.00, Rosenheim, Germany,; Himmler, 7 October 1900, 16.28, Munich, Germany .
[5] More precisely, the degree of the sign.

Chapter 4
[6] The original just mentions 1984 conjunction
[7] Liberal Party, the main UK political reforming force in the Houses of Parliament at this time, is omitted in the original French
[8] Also, world government bail outs of banking industries, encouraged by the Piscean British Prime Minister, Gordon Brown, can be seen as a manifestation of this Jupiter/Neptune conjunction!

Chapter 5
[9] Original French reads: Ne nous étonnons pas non plus que l'attentat aux USA du 11 septembre 2001, accompagné d'opposition périphérique de Mars, soit survenu alors que Pluton recevait une double opposition de Jupiter et Saturne.

Chapter 7
[10] The original French refers generally to the year's Jupiter opposition to Saturn, Uranus and Neptune. At the time of the Beijing Spring, Jupiter had not reached this position, but was in a wide quincunx to it. However, and most significantly, the other three planets had or were opposing the party triple conjunction. So I have noted this in the text.
[11] The 2026 chart overleaf and what follows is new material supplied by the author for this English edition.

Chapter 8
[12] And 1947 is generally accepted to be the beginning of the Cold War.
[13] By the French 'triangle harmonique', we assume André is referring to the sextile, semi-sextile configuration between Saturn, Uranus and Pluto building in December 1978 .

[14] This section has been re-written to explain, in a little more detail than in the original French, the connection between Mars' special position in its cycle and the Saturn/Pluto opposition. André describes the importance of the Mars perigee more fully at the end of Chapter 15.

[15] Editor's note: In addition to AIDs, 1981-83 saw the advent of monetarism and the consequential path to globalization, as well as Middle East instability – all of which could well be the root issues behind what André now goes on to consider will be the issues of 2020-23, when the three planets, then in Capricorn, are together again

Chapter 9
[16] It is often pointed out that Uranus was in Gemini at this time, very close to its position in the early 1940s when electronic computers were starting to be used. The consequential dimensional social changes later in both centuries are remarkably similar.

[17] In Sagittarius/Capricorn 1988-90.

Chapter 10
[18] Saturn passed across Uranus and Pluto on the cusp of Taurus mid-1851 and its retrogression kept it in close orb for nearly a year after this.

[19] What follows are the original words written in advanced of events.

Chapter 11
[20] Those years saw the Neptune-Pluto conjunction in a T-square to Jupiter and Uranus moving to a Jupiter- Neptune- Pluto conjunction opposed by Saturn taking the place of Uranus.

[21] That is, was in orb.

[22] Unique French word that means the astro-influenced human body.

Chapter 14
[23] The indicator's sharp fall clearly reflects the Soviet collapse, via the Gulf War down to the early 1990s recession and then the boom to the end of the century. The 'decline in popular democracies' may have been caused by this boom, but it did not become apparent until the 21st century – which is covered later in the chapter.

Chapter 15
[24] André comments that similar cases were Nicholas I of Russia and George VI in United Kingdom leading to Elizabeth II, who succeeded him.

[25] That is, started a chain of events.

[26] This addition was submitted in French by André in October 2015,, to translate and add to the English edition. Although the period described will be passing around the planned publication date, it will be interesting for readers in the future to look back and compare notes with what happened at this time.

Chapter 17
[27] Pierre Simon Laplace, *A Philosophical Essay on Probabilities.* Original translation from the author's French quotation.

Index

AIDS 112, 121, 144, 149, 164
Apocalypse 67
Arab world 42, 84, 144
Artificial insemination 122
AstroCartoGraphy 45
Austro-Prussian War 23
Authoritarian(ism) 23, 71
B
Balkan War(s) 29, 77, 119, 148
Beijing Spring 99, 100, 163
Berlin Wall 15, 16, 37, 74, 80, 81, 89, 100, 121, 149, 150
Bin Laden 110, 162
Biotechnology 137
Boer War 26, 125
Bolshevik(s/ism) 46, 88, 91, 92, 93
   and Mensheviks 91
Bosnian crisis 29, 77
Boston Tea Party 86
Boulangism 24, 119
Boxer Rebellion 26, 125
Kellogg-Briand Pact 31, 58
British
   Empire 19, 125
   Imperialism 18, 72
   Monarchy 17
C
Camp David 96
Capitalism 59, 74, 75, 93, 120, 126, 130, 145
   Neo- 74, 82
Chaldeans 159
Christian(ity) 5, 17, 18, 114, 159
Colonialism 41, 42, 68, 124, 125
Cominform 94
Common Market 34, 35, 61
Communism(/t) 14, 36, 55, 69, 79, 81, 82, 88, 89, 92-95, 98-101, 106, 108, 118, 120, 134, 145
   Manifesto 47, 87, 118

Contraception 44, 69, 122
Council of Europe 33, 36, 37
Cuban Missile Crisis 42, 96
D
De-colonialization 88
Decolonization 95, 106, 120, 125, 127, 143
Demilitarization 32, 97, 120
Democracy(/ies/tic/tize) 23, 33, 52-56, 58-60, 73, 74, 89, 90, 94, 98, 100, 118, 119, 121, 149, 164
Democratization 118
Dictatorship 33-37
   Communist 69
   Nazi 33, 73, 78
   Soviet 92
   Stalinist 92, 95
Disarmament Conference 31, 54, 58
DNA 44, 137
Dolly the Sheep 137
Dumbarton Oaks Conference 140
E
East India Company 71, 124
Economic
   Crisis 5, 31, 36, 51, 64, 65, 76-78, 81, 89, 93, 134, 148-150
   Expansionism 78
   Growth 82, 83, 150,
   Unification 34
Egyptian-Soviet Friendship Treaty 97
Eisenhower Doctrine 80
Electricity 39, 40, 51, 113, 114
Electronic innovation 51
El Niño 137
Emancipation of Labour 88, 90
Napoleon, Emperor 20-23, 72, 74, 75, 86, 117
Alexander the Great 117
Entente Cordiale 22, 28, 53, 56, 77
Ethiopian War 32, 59

European Atomic Energy
Community 34
European Coal and Steel
Community 33
European
   Community 32, 34, 35, 66, 80, 101
     Council (in Brussels) 35, 37
     Defence Community 33
     Economic Community 34, 36, 37
     Federal Union 58
     Monetary crisis 35, 80
     Soviet Empire 102
     Union 33, 34, 36, 38
Europeanization 41, 75, 124
Explorer 1 128

F
Fabian Society 88, 90
Falklands War 42, 70
Fascist(/m) 31, 54, 76, 78, 113, 144,
Feudal(ism) 17, 39, 130
First World War 27, 31, 39, 41, 54, 77, 88, 105, 119, 143, 148
French Revolution 20, 39, 40, 46, 52, 154

G
Genetically Modified Organisms (GMO) 135
Genocide
   Cambodian 112
   Rwandan 70
Global Europeanization 124
Globalization 81, 82, 121, 135, 136, 146, 147, 164
   Anti- 82, 83
Gorbachev, Mikhail 55, 62, 99, 100
Great Conjunction 11, 100, 116, 129, 141, 145
Great Depression 150
Great Year 11, 17, 151, 159-161
Greenpeace 55
Gulf Crisis 149

H
Hanoverian dynasty 72
Hiltler(ism) 14, 31-33, 45, 59, 64-67, 73, 74, 94, 149, 156, 163
   Führer, the 64, 113, 141
Hindus 159
Hundred Years War 17

I
Imperialist(/m) 18, 25, 41, 71-77, 129-131, 144
Industrial Revolution 51, 74, 105, 117, 125
Inflation 75, 81
Information technology 51, 121, 144, 146
International Geophysical Year 128
International Monetary System 82
Internet 42, 44, 51, 74, 82, 129, 135, 136, 150
Islam(ic) 17, 70, 122, 123

J
Japanese
   Naval disaster 142
   Revolution 53
Jihad 70
Jurassic Park 70

K
Kamikaze attack 110, 158
KGB 100
Korean War 79, 106, 120, 149, 150
Kremlin 59, 101
Kulturkampf 23
Kyoto
   Convention 56, 57
   Protocol 136

L
League of Nations 30, 31, 54, 56-59, 78, 120, 130
Lebensraum policy 66
Lend-Lease 60
Lenin 54, 56, 91, 92
Lysenko affair 95

Index

M
Maastricht Treaty 37
Mao Tse-tung 94, 97, 106, 108
Médecins Sans Frontières 55
Mexican War 75
Middle Ages 159
Middle East 34, 42, 80, 97, 106, 125, 164
Millennium) 17, 113, 124, 132, 159
Mobile phone 51, 121, 129, 135, 136
Moon landing 39, 97
Motor car 97
Free Trade Agreement of the Americas (NAFTA) 135
World Trade Organization (WTO) 82, 135
N
Nationalism 21, 86, 135
Nazi(s/sm) 30-33, 45, 46, 58, 61, 64, 65, 67, 78, 94, 120, 134, 142
Neo-Platonists 159
Neutrality Act 60
Nobel Prize 10, 96
Non-Governmental
O
Organisations (NGOs) 136
Organisation for Economic Co-operation and Development (OECD) 136, 149
Oil 35, 36, 51, 69, 112, 126, 150
Organization of the Petroleum Exporting Countries (OPEC) 35
Ostpolitik 55
Ottoman
   Empire 53
   Turks 18
Outer Space Treaty 97
P
Pandemic 110-112, 151
Paris Pact 31, 58

Peace Treaty of Aix-la-Chapelle 20, 71
People's Republic of China 100, 106
Perigee 110, 158, 164
Perihelion 43, 110, 158
Palestine Liberation Organization (PLO) 69, 109
Polish Communist Party 98
Poverty 64, 85, 103, 111
Prague Spring 97
Proletariat 92, 118
Prometheus 113
R
Race riots 80
Reagan, Ronald 55, 62, 81
Red Army 66, 94, 97, 98, 140, 141
Renaissance 17, 114, 159
   Italian 18
Retrograde 43, 118
Roman Empire 17
Rommel 67, 140, 141
S
Second World War 41, 48, 54, 60, 73, 78, 106, 130, 139, 141, 143, 148-150, 155
Sexual revolution 69, 122
Space race 96, 97
Spanish revolution 93
Sputnik 96, 128
Stalin 5, 88, 92, 93, 95, 96, 101, 156
   De-Stalinisation 95-96
Suez Crisis 34
T
Technology revolution 51, 67, 74, 117
Terrorism(/t) 69, 83, 109, 110, 112, 121, 127, 144, 158
Third Reich 59, 73, 142, 156, 157
Third world 42, 68, 69, 88, 95, 96, 110, 112, 125, 134, 149
Thirty Years War 17
Tsunami 131

U
Union of Soviet Socialist Republics (USSR) 32, 41, 58-61, 78, 79, 81, 92-101, 140, 156
United Nations (UN) 54, 56, 57, 59, 61, 79

V
Vietnam War 80, 107

W
Watergate 81
Women's liberation 144
Working class 54, 89, 90, 93, 102
World Trade Centre 110
World Trade Organisation (WTO) 82, 135

Y
Yom Kippur War 109, 120

Order *The Value of Astrology* at:
http://astrologicalassociation.com/shop/books/barbault.html
Email:office@astrologicalassociation.,com

The first book available in English by this great French master astrologer; The Value of Astrology offers incisive, captivating insights into the origins, classical tradition and modern uses of astrology.

'Will Astrology be taken seriously at last?'

The book includes

- Andre's famous pioneering and rigorous understanding of mundane astrology.
- An incisive outline of its historical and philosophical importance.
- Beautiful insight into its relationship with psychology and painting.
- Clear summaries of attempts to assess astrology statistically.

Drawing on Andre's nearly 80 years with astrology, here is a special opportunity to touch the wisdom of an exceptional human being, who justifiably shows there are irresistible cultural, statistical and mundane reasons to claim, 'Astrology should be taken seriously at last'.

'When the history of twentieth century European astrology is finally written, André Barbault will be given an honoured place: over the course of his life Barbault has encountered most of the major astrologers in Europe, including C.G.Jung. This book includes some of his most important writing on astrology's value, nature and significance, developed over more than half-a-century of study, and available for the first time in English.'
Nicholas Campion, author of *A History of Western Astrology*

'Andre has a very special style in French and I can hear his voice in the way Kate chose to translate... What a good job she's done! ......Reading Andre Barbault in French many years ago, brought one of the great astrological awakenings of my life. Now, reading him in English for the first time, I am dazzled again. .. In this book, you will meet one of the most original and inventive astrologers of the 20th century.' **Lynn Bell**

'[I am]....so familiar with Barbault's prolific work [in French], this publication is truly impressive as it seems to pull together a life of experience in a succinct volume. It is time for the English speaking world to get a glimpse of this master astrologer.' **Monica Domino**

ISBN 978-0-9502658-8-9

£15.00
Published by The Astrological Association

André Barbault

Aperçu astrologique sur l'amour

Éd. lulu.com
Mai 2013

André Barbault

La Seconde Guerre mondiale

Astrologie

Éd. lulu.com
Mai 2014

www.ingramcontent.com/pod-product-compliance
Lightning Source LLC
Chambersburg PA
CBHW062223080426
42734CB00010B/2002